The Book of Candle Making:
Creating Scent, Beauty & Light

The Book of
Candlemaking

Chris Larkin

Sterling Publishing Co., Inc.
New York
A STERLING/CHAPELLE BOOK

For Chapelle Ltd.

Owner: Jo Packham

Editor: Karmen Potts Quinney

Staff: Marie Barber, Areta Bingham, Malissa Boatwright, Kass Burchett, Rebecca Christensen, Marilyn Goff, Shirley Heslop, Holly Hollingsworth, Susan Jorgensen, Pauline Locke, Ginger Mikkelsen, Barbara Milburn, Linda Orton, Leslie Ridenour, and Cindy Stoeckl

Designers: Joy Anckner, Holly Fuller, Amber Hansen, Kelly Henderson, Jamie Pierce, Rhonda Rainey, and Cindy Rooks

Photographer: Kevin Dilley for Hazen Photography Studio

Photography Stylists: Susan Laws and Leslie Liechty

Library of Congress Cataloging-in-Publication Data

Larkin, Chris.
   The book of candlemaking : creating scent, beauty & light / Chris Larkin.
      p.   cm.
   "A Sterling/Chapelle book."
   Includes index.
   ISBN 0-8069-0676-6
   1. Candlemaking.   I. Title.
TT896.5.L37   1997   97-41180
745.593'32—dc21   CIP

A Sterling/Chapelle Book

10 9 8 7 6 5 4 3

First paperback edition published in 1999 by
Sterling Publishing Company, Inc.
387 Park Avenue South, New York, N.Y. 10016
Originally published in hard cover as *Candle Making*
© 1998 by Chapelle Limited
Distributed in Canada by Sterling Publishing
% Canadian Manda Group, One Atlantic Avenue, Suite 105
Toronto, Ontario, Canada M6K 3E7
Distributed in Great Britain and Europe by Cassell PLC
Wellington House, 125 Strand, London WC2R 0BB, England
Distributed in Australia by Capricorn Link (Australia) Pty Ltd.
P.O. Box 6651, Baulkham Hills, Business Centre, NSW 2153,
Australia
Printed and bound in China
All rights reserved

Sterling ISBN 0-8069-0676-6 Trade
            0-8069-7787-6 Paper

Several projects shown in this publication were created with the outstanding and innovative products developed by A.I. Root Company, Ambiance, Anita's, Barker Candle Supplies, Bucilla, Personal Stamp Exchange, Caron Collection, Delta, Eclectic Corporation, Modern Masters, Plaid, and Walnut Hill.

   We would like to offer our sincere appreciation for the valuable support given in this ever changing industry of new ideas, concepts, designs, and products.

   Due to the limited amount of space available, we must print our patterns at a reduced size in order to give our patrons the maximum number of patterns possible in our publications. We believe the quality and quantity of our patterns will compensate for any inconvenience this may cause.

   If you have any questions or comments or would like information on specialty products featured in this book, please contact: Chapelle Ltd., Inc.,
P.O. Box 9252 Ogden, UT 84409
(801) 621-2777 • FAX (801) 621-2788

Table of Contents

An Introduction to Candle Making

Candles are more than just a source of light. For centuries they have been used for symbolic and religious purposes. Candles also serve as a focal point for celebrations throughout the world.

The first candles, tallow candles, were made from beef or mutton fat. These candles produced black smoke and a greasy smell. Beeswax offered a more decorative and better smelling candle. However, with the cost of beeswax being so high, only the rich or clergy could use these higher quality candles. Eventually, the development of stearin and paraffin increased the availability of decorative and scented candles.

Through the centuries, the materials needed to create candles have advanced, while the method of

creating a candle has stayed the same. Although candles are no longer a necessity for light, their popularity is enormous. They are still used for symbolic and religious reasons. However, the use of candles in today's society has a much broader spectrum. Candles are a very versatile item. Some offer healing and relaxation through their scent. Others contain a scent that repels mosquitoes. The variety of colors and shapes in which they are available add to their simple and timeless beauty. Candles can add a unique touch to any type of setting. Their flickering light seems to draw people together. The look of a room can be enhanced simply by the way a candle is used.

Candle making can produce so many unique results. The step-by-step instructions with pictures featured in this book are easy to follow. Create the simplest to the most complicated candles using the items that are available in today's market.

Candles come in a variety of colors, shapes, sizes, and scents. With this book as a guide, candles such as molded, double mold, dipped candles, rolled candles, and floating candles can be made by anyone. Acquire skills such as carving, pinching, and twisting to create one-of-a-kind candles. Learn how to decorate candles using techniques such as découpaging, embossing, and leafing.

Candle holders and containers are an important part of the way a candle is used and displayed. Learn easy and creative ways to decorate candle holders and containers with fabric, beads, and paint. Keep in mind that many household items can be turned into candle holders and containers.

Page after page offers fun and elegant ways to illuminate both purchased candles and those created from scratch. Discover contemporary ideas for decorating with candles and containers, creating a relaxed and intimate atmosphere.

Creating the finished projects shown in this book may take some experimenting and practice. However, once the basic techniques of candle making and decorating are mastered, the possibilities of creating scent, beauty, and light are endless.

The finished candles shown in Chapter Four: Candle Making are purchased candles. Purchased candles were used to better show a greater variety of possible results.

7

What is to Follow

The following outline will briefly explain each chapter in this book. Please read all relevant instructions before beginning any project.

Chapter One: Become familiar with the equipment and supplies needed for candle making.

Chapter Two: Learn about the ingredients needed to make candles, such as the different types of waxes and hardeners required.

Chapter Three: Gain knowledge on candle making safety. Learn how to melt wax. Become familiar with candle making clean-up.

Chapter Four: Select desired type of candle. Read all instructions for that candle. View the photograph of the desired candle following the project instructions.

Gather needed equipment and supplies. See Chapter Three if candle requires melting wax. Read instructions carefully. Begin.

Chapter Five: Acquire knowledge on ways to decorate candles and candle containers for holidays and celebrations. Gather needed equipment and supplies. Read instructions carefully. Begin.

Chapter Six: Learn different techniques for decorating purchased candles and those created from scratch. Gather needed equipment and supplies. Read instructions carefully. Begin.

Chapter Seven: Learn ways to embellish candle holders and containers using simple techniques and household items. Gather needed equipment and supplies. Read instructions carefully. Begin.

Chapter Eight: See creative and elegant ways to display candles in any setting. Learn how to make beautiful ice candles that make a wonderful centerpiece at any party.

Chapter One:
Equipment and Supplies

Most of the equipment and supplies needed for making candles may not need to be purchased. Many of the items may already be in the home.

Container

Use any type of an appropriate-sized container for holding the water bath when using metal molds.

Double Boiler

Use a double boiler for melting the wax. It should be made of stainless steel or aluminum. Make certain the water in the bottom pan does not boil dry. Fill with more water as necessary. Once the molten wax has been poured, wipe around the inside of the double boiler with a dry kitchen towel to clean. *Note: A container inside of a frying pan or pan filled with water can easily be substituted for a double boiler as shown in photo. A rack or trivet can be placed between the container and pan. A metal chain can be used to hold the container down in the boiling water.*

Funnel

Use a funnel to refill molds.

Hammer

Use a hammer to break wax blocks into smaller pieces.

Heating Element

Use either a stove, or hot plate.

Measuring Device

Use a scale to properly weigh the required amount of wax. If a scale is not available, break the blocks of wax into even segments by scoring with a ruler and pushing an ice pick into the wax every inch or so along the scored lines. For example, a ten pound block broken into five equal pieces yields two pound pieces of wax.

Measuring Spoons

Use measuring spoons to measure ingredients such as oils and dyes.

Melting Pot

Use any type of metal can, such as an empty coffee can, to hold wax for melting.

Molds

Use desired type of glass, plastic, household, rubber, or metal mold in desired shape and size, from simple geometrics to ornate fruits and flowers.

Newspapers

Cover the work surface with plenty of paper for easy clean-up.

Pan

Choose a pan large enough to accommodate the melting pot.

Paper Towels

Use paper towels to wipe wax from equipment while still warm.

Paring Knife

Use a sharp paring knife to trim the seam lines from the candle, cut wicks to length, and for carving.

Pliers

Use pliers to lift and remove the melting pot from the pan and to hold the melting pot while pouring.

Pot Holders

Use pot holders for safely handling hot materials. Hot containers may be rested upon pot holders also.

Alternative Method

11

Probe

Use a long knitting needle, pointed dowel, or metal skewer to stir in scent or dye. The sharp end of the probe is also used to poke down into the center of the candle to open the wax around the wick.

Trivet or Rack

Create a safe homemade alternative to the double boiler by placing a trivet or rack inside the pan with the water deep enough to come at least halfway up the sides of the melting pot. Punch holes in a 6¼"-diameter metal lid for a quick and easy handmade trivet.

Wax Glue

Use to adhere pieces of wax together or to adhere embellishments to a candle. It is a soft, sticky wax. It is available in solid form and is melted in very small amounts in the top of a double boiler.

Wax Thermometer

Wax must be heated to certain temperatures when making candles. A candy or cooking thermometer may be used as long as the gauge covers the same scale as a wax thermometer which is 38-108°C (100-225°F). Closely watch the temperature when melting wax and never leave melting wax unattended as it is as volatile as hot cooking oil.

Waxed Paper or Aluminum Foil

Cover newspaper with waxed paper or aluminum foil to keep spilled wax clean. Spilled wax may be peeled from the waxed paper or aluminum foil and remelted.

Weights

Wax is lighter than water. To prevent a filled mold from floating in a water bath, use lead weights or a length of chain to anchor the mold.

Wicking Needle

Use wicking needles (4-10" in length) to insert wicks and to secure wicks at the base of the mold.

Types of Wicks

A wick is what makes the wax a candle. Wicks must be carefully chosen to ensure proper burning. There are four types of wicks: flat, floating, square, and wire core. Wicks, usually made of braided cotton and specially treated to slow the burning rate, come in a variety of types and sizes and are sold in spools or small packages. They are chosen according to the size and type of candle.

Flat Wicks are generally used for dipping candles.

Floating Wicks are for floating candles.

Square Wicks are for poured candles.

Wire Core Wicks are for container and votive candles.

Using Wicks

The size of the wick depends upon the diameter of the candle being made. An inch of wick is needed for each diameter inch. Use fatter wicks for larger candles. For a tall container, place primed wick on a wick tab into bottom center of container. Pour melted wax while holding onto wick. For a short container, pour wax and let it harden. Using a needle, poke a hole through the center of the wick. Insert wick. For a medium container, pour wax and let it cool until a thick film forms over surface. Insert primed wick on wick tab into candle.

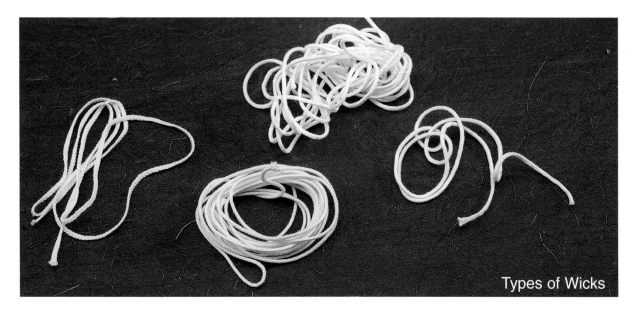

Types of Wicks

Keep wicks trimmed to ½"-1". Allow wicks to cool before trimming and re-lighting. When extinguishing the candle flame, dip the wick into the melted wax and straighten it immediately. This keeps the wick free of soot and prevents it from smoking.

Primed Wicks are wicks that have been treated. To prime an unprimed wick, soak it in melted wax for five minutes. Remove coated wick and lay straight on waxed paper to dry.

Wick Tabs are small, flat metal discs used to anchor the wick in container candles. The wick is pushed through the hole in the disc and the prongs are pinched together to firmly hold wick.

Pinching Wick Tab

Tips for Wicks

◼ Always soak wick in hot wax before using it. Dip wick in hot wax and pull it straight as wax cools.

◼ Never let water get on the wick unless it is heavily waxed before. Water will stop the wax from penetrating the threads, and this can cause irregular burning or spluttering of flame.

◼ Ensure that the wick is always centered in a candle, otherwise the candle burns lopsidedly and soon loses its shape.

Chapter Two:
Ingredients

Ingredients for candles vary depending on the type, color, and scent of the candle. However, most candles require the same basic ingredients. The most essential ingredient in a candle is wax. The type of wax used will effect the final look of the candle.

Types of Wax

There are four types of wax typically used for candle making. They are paraffin, beeswax, bead wax, and stearin.

Paraffin Wax is the basic wax used for candle making. It contains oil, is colorless and odorless, and has a glossy, translucent finish when hardened. It is sold by weight and may be purchased in bead, block, or pellet form.

Paraffin wax is generally classified by melting points such as low (126°-132°F), medium (135°-145°F), and high (145°-150°F). Low-melt waxes are used for container candles, votives, and cut-and-

curl candles. Medium-melt waxes are used for general candle making, dipped candles, and floating candles. High-melt waxes are used for specialized candle making such as hurricane candles. Paraffin wax drips too much when used alone, so often stearin is added to the wax. Vibar, available at candle making shops, may be substituted for stearin, or paraffin wax premixed with stearin may be found at candle making shops.

Beeswax is an all-natural product and slightly more expensive than paraffin wax. It is available in shades of brown or bleached white, and several other colors. It has a sweet honey scent. It, too, is sold by weight and may be purchased in block, pellet, or sheet form. It is generally combined with other waxes to increase burning time and improve the wax for molding and dipping.

Beeswax is very sticky, so candles made just from beeswax generally need to be dipped or rolled. If molds

are used, a special releasing agent must first be applied. Due to its low-shrinkage qualities, few or no wells form in the middle of the candle which means little or no refilling as the candle cools.

Ingredients

Place wick and wick tab into bottom of container. Make certain it is centered. Spoon bead wax into container of choice for burning and displaying candle.

Spooning Bead Wax

Stearin, made from commercial stearic acid, is quite harmless to touch, and will not damage surfaces or clothes. When it is sold for candle making it is usually mixed with other materials. It acts like beeswax or paraffin.

A pure stearin candle can be made; however, it is mostly used in conjunction with other waxes. It has important uses in candle making. It is harder and less easily softened by heat. When added to another wax, it will make candles that stand up in hot conditions without sagging. It helps candles come away from molds easily.

Stearin is whiter than paraffin. It is also a good solvent for dyes. Colors will appear brighter when used. From 3-5 tablespoons of stearin are added directly to each pound of wax as it is being melted. Measure carefully as excess stearin will cause a soap-like finish on the candle. Water-cooling is recommended when stearin has been used, because air-cooling produces a mottled appearance.

Types of Hardeners

Opaque and Translucent Crystals act as wax hardeners. Both types of crystals have very high melting points (above 200°F) and must first be carefully melted in a small pan with a small amount of wax over direct heat before being added to the larger pot of wax. Only ½ to 1 teaspoon of crystals is needed for each pound of wax. In addition to hardening the wax, both types of crystals increase the burning time of candles and produce a lustrous finish.

Opaque crystals whiten the wax, make colors very clear, and produce a glossy finish.

Bead Wax is wax that has been granulated into small beads. It can be found in a variety of colors and scents. Bead wax can be mixed or layered for a colorful candle. The items needed to create a bead wax candle are: bead wax, spoon, container (glass, metal or ceramic) wick, and wick tab.

Translucent crystals help retain the natural translucency of the wax and make colors have a glass-like appearance. Translucent crystals are always needed when making hurricane candles.

Dye

Dyes allow wax to be shaded in a wide spectrum of colors. Dyes can make candles more attractive to use, decorate with, and give as gifts.

Dyes are sold in concentrated colored wax squares in a variety of colors. Each square colors about a pound of wax. Use more squares for deeper colors. Mix squares to get an endless variety of colors. Crayons are not recommended because crayon pigment clogs the wick and prevents the candle from burning properly.

The amount of dye used depends upon the shade desired. Test the color by pouring a small amount of molten wax that has been colored onto waxed paper and allowing it to cool. The color will be slightly lighter than the finished candle. Always increase the color gradually, building the color from light to dark.

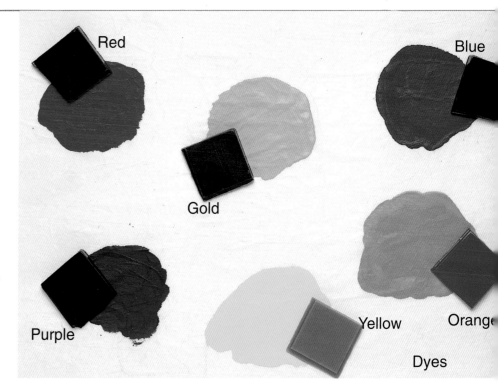

Be careful when using any type of dye. Clothes and some plastic equipment can become permanently dyed. Do not put too much color into the mixture.

Tips for Dyes

- Do not use clear wax when making a black candle. Use old scrap wax and then add the needed amount of black. Too much black dye can affect the candle's burning qualities.

- Do not overheat any wax containing blue dyes or other colors that contain blues such as green or purple. Too much heat will cause discoloration at the time of heating or within a short time after.

- Do not put too much color into the mixture. Over-dyed wax does not glow well when the candle is lit.

Types of Scents

Scents may be added to candle wax to give off an aroma while burning. After the wax has reached the right temperature for pouring and once it has been removed from the heat. The scent is added and stirred well. It is added last to keep evaporation to a minimum. Be careful not to add too much scent as this may cause mottling or pitting and make releasing from the mold difficult. An alternative to scenting the wax is to scent the wick by saturating it in scent before the priming process. Scents are available in solid wax perfume squares, liquid forms or natural herbs.

Solid Wax Perfume Squares come in a variety of scents. The perfume square is placed into the melted wax.

Liquid Forms must be oil-based because oil is the only compatible base for a wax candle. Therefore, if using perfume, make certain the perfume is oil-based and not alcohol-based. It takes only a small amount (3-5 drops) to scent a pound of wax.

Natural Herbs can be fresh or dried. Natural scented candles produce rich and soft scents. Natural scents are believed to cleanse the mind and soul. To make natural scented candles, stir fresh herbs into melted wax

Types of Scents

and maintain a temperature of 180°F for 45 minutes. Remove herbs using a slotted spoon as shown below. (If herbs are left in wax at this stage, when candle is made they will sink to the bottom of candle. Also, herbs become flammable when candle is lit.)

Removing Herbs

Make desired candle. See Chapter Four: Candle Making on pages 22-48.

Natural Candle Scents
Allspice
Cinnamon
Clove
Eucalyptus
Jasmine
Lavender
Pine
Rose

Aromatherapy uses essential oils to help balance the human body and work in harmony with nature. These oils are extracted from plants shrubs, trees, flowers, seeds, roots, and grasses. These oils contain the essential life force of plants. When these oils are blended, they create some very enjoyable and effective products. These oils should be used in small amounts. Essential oils have a one year shelf life.

When making a candle, add essential oils after wax has melted. See Chapter Three: Melting Wax on pages 19-21. For information on what effects the different scents have, see Aromatic Effects on page 47.

Essential oils can also be added to unscented purchased candles. See instructions on page 47.

Tips for Essential Oils

■ Be careful not to get essential oils or their strong vapors in the eyes. If this does happen, flush the eyes with cool water.

■ Do not consume alcohol (other than a glass of wine with a meal) when using essential oils.

■ Take extra care when using essential oils, if pregnant.

■ Use caution with essential oils, as they tend to irritate the skin.

■ Do not use essential oils, if on medication.

■ Store essential oils out of sight and reach of children.

■ Store essential oils in a dark place. Light and oxygen cause essential oils to deteriorate at a fast rate.

■ Do not spill essential oils on furniture or clothes. Oils may leave stains.

Chapter Three:
Melting Wax

Safety for Candle Making and Usage

- Always use a thermometer when melting wax.

- Never leave melting wax unattended. Unlike water, wax does not boil. It gets hotter and hotter until it flashes into a flame.

- Never use water to put out a wax fire. Smother the fire with baking soda.

- If wax comes in contact with skin, bathe the area immediately in cold water. Peel off the wax and treat burned area as any other burn or scald.

- Never pour molten wax down the drain.

- Do not add drops of scent to a burning candle.

- Keep wicks trimmed to avoid large flames and smoking.

- Burn candles away from any drafts.

- Keep candles out of strong light. It causes them to fade.

- Burn candles upright in a container or holder. Never burn a candle by it self, because a fire can easily occur.

- Do not put any debris, such as burnt matches or wicks, into candles. It can cause a fire.

- Do not leave burning candles unattended, especially when children and pets are nearby.

Melting Wax

Allow approximately 1½ - 4 hours for wax to melt, depending upon the size of the container and the temperature of the heating element.

Things Needed
- Ingredients on pages 14-18
- Double boiler
- Hammer
- Heating element
- Mold/container of desired candle
- Screwdriver
- Thermometer
- Water

Instructions

1. Calculate amount of wax needed (for the mold/container of desired candle) by filling the mold/ container with water and measuring it – 3 ounces of cold wax are needed for every 3½ fluid ounces of water.

2. Break wax into small pieces using hammer and screwdriver.

Things Needed

Step 2

3. Put wax pieces into top of double boiler or melting pot.

4. Fill bottom portion of double boiler with water, or place the melting pot into the sauce pan and fill with enough water to come halfway up the sides of the melting pot.

5. Set double boiler or pan on the heating element. Make certain water does not boil dry. Place thermometer in

wax, making certain thermometer bulb does not touch the bottom of the pan.

Step 5

6. Turn heat on medium low. If water begins to boil rapidly, reduce heat to a gentle boil to prevent water from splashing into the container. Make certain heat is not reduced too much, as doing so will cause difficulty in keeping the temperature accurate.

7. Once wax is melted and is at the specified temperature, add hardener (if necessary), dye, and scent. This may lower the temperature. Make certain wax is brought back up to the temperature needed.

8. Make desired candle. See Chapter Four: Candle Making on pages 22-48 for making different types of candles.

Tea Light Candles can be created in any desired color. Fill tea light container with colored melted wax. Let wax cool. Pierce a hole through center of candle with a heated large-eyed needle. Place primed wick in hole.

Tips for Clean-Up

■ Pour excess wax into an old pan lined with greaseproof waxed paper. DO NOT pour wax down the drain. It will clog the drain. Let wax set and set aside for reuse at a later date.

■ Place equipment in boiling water until wax melts. Wipe away wax using a paper towel and then wash equipment in warm, soapy water. Or, let equipment soak in a basin filled with hot water and a degreasing detergent.

■ Place metal molds in a 150°F oven on a foil-lined cookie sheet and heat for 15 minutes. Wax will melt and run onto foil. DO NOT heat oven higher than 150°F — a higher temperature will cause the welds in the molds to melt.

■ Discard old cans, lids, and other replaceable equipment.

■ If desired, purchase a candle cleaning kit from a candle making store to aid in removing stubborn stains and wax build-up.

■ Rather than prying and scraping melted wax from glass containers and votive holders, place them in a freezer. Wax will shrink and easily pop out.

■ If wax spills onto clothing or cloth, pour hot water onto the spill to melt away wax.

■ If wax spills onto carpet, allow wax to harden and then rub with an ice cube. Wax will become brittle and can then be easily scraped up with a dull knife. Any remaining residue can be cleaned up with repeated treatments using a hot, damp cloth or sponge.

Chapter Four:
Candle Making

Molded Candles

Most candlemakers' suppliers and craft shops can supply a range of molds ready to use. Simple molds tend to display various hues and textures of the wax most effectively.

Molds are available in an endless variety of shapes and sizes, from simple geometrics to ornate fruits and flowers. Molds are relatively in-expensive, and their sturdiness allows for long-lasting, repeated use. They are made of metal, plastic, rubber, or acrylic. Glass is also suitable for molds, but it is most often used in casting since the mold must be broken to remove the candle.

Many household cartons and containers make excellent molds, too. Anything that can be pulled, peeled, or broken off from the finished candle works well. Some examples are: canning jars, cartons, frozen juice containers,

Molds and Molding Supplies

milk cartons, galvanized buckets, margarine tubs, small paper cups, terra-cotta pots, and yogurt containers.

Mold Seals are made from reusable, sticky, putty-like material used for making acrylic molds watertight. They are firmly pressed over the taped wick on the bottom of a mold, and can also be used to secure the wick in a mold. Make certain any seal residue is removed from the wick — even the smallest amount will keep the wick from burning. Make certain to use plenty of mold seal to make the mold airtight.

Ideas for Mold Shapes

- Animals
- Blocks
- Eggs
- Fish
- Flowers
- Fruits
- Moons
- Pillar
- Pyramid
- Vegetables
- Stars

Pouring Temperatures

Mold Material	Range (°F)
Acrylic molds	180°-210°
Candy molds (plastic)	160°
Clay molds	180°-210°
Dipping candles	155°-160°
Glass molds	170°-200°
Metal molds	180°-210°
Plaster molds	160°-180°
Rubber molds	160°-180°
Sand candles (sand off)	155°-160°
Sand candles (sand on)	270°-280°
Tear-away molds	160°

Tips for Molded Candles

▪ Make certain wax contains at least 10 percent stearin, whether the wax is premixed or not. Add additional stearin if necessary. The stearin increases the amount of shrinkage, making the candle slip easily from the mold. If using beeswax, make certain a releasing agent has been applied to the mold.

▪ Remove dust and unwanted particles from molds by simply blowing them out.

▪ Once the mold is clean and dry, apply a coat of silicone spray to the inside of the mold. A light application of vegetable oil is also suitable for coating the mold.

▪ Use a generous amount of mold seal to ensure the mold is watertight.

▪ When possible, use a water bath to reduce the amount of time needed for cooling. Candles may be cooled at room temperature but water-cooling improves the appearance.

▪ To speed the final cooling process, put the candle in the refrigerator and remove it as soon as it is cold to the touch. Tiny cracks and lines may appear if the candle is allowed to cool longer than necessary.

Things Needed

- Ingredients on pages 14-18
- Aluminum foil
- Container
- Double boiler
- Dowel
- Funnel
- Fry pan
- Mold
- Mold release, silicone spray, or vegetable oil
- Mold seal
- Paper towels
- Probe
- Scissors: craft
- Sharp knife
- Straight pin
- Wax thermometer
- Weight
- Wick: square, primed

Things Needed

Instructions

1. Clean and dry the mold and then coat with mold release, silicone spray, or vegetable oil.

2. Turn mold upside down. Thread a primed wick through the hole in the base of the mold and up through to the top of the mold.

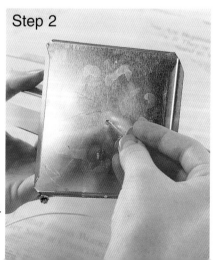
Step 2

3. Turn mold upright and wrap wick around the dowel.

Step 3

4. Turn mold upside down again and pull the wick taut, without stretching it. Slip a straight pin through wick so it crosses the hole and lays against bottom of mold.

Step 4

5. Cut wick to a ½" length. Bunch it up close to the hole and cover it with mold seal, making certain the hole is watertight.

6. Determine amount of wax needed for the mold and melt wax following instructions for Melting Wax on pages 19-21.

7. Pour wax into center of mold being careful not to splash wax onto the sides of the mold. Fill metal molds to within ½" of the top and fill acrylic and two-piece plastic molds to the top.

Step 7

8. Check to make certain wick is still centered. Set remaining wax aside for refilling, keeping it heated to the same temperature.

9. Allow wax to set for several minutes and then gently tap side of mold.

10. Set acrylic and plastic molds aside on a level surface to cool. Cool metal molds in a water bath to insure a clear, glossy finish. Immerse mold to within ½" of the top in a container filled with lukewarm water, making certain water does not splash onto wax. Place a heavy object over top of mold to keep it from floating. *Note: A depression will form around wick as candle cools. Wax hardens from the bottom up and from the outside in. Simultaneously, it hardens across the top, causing the depression and a cavity in candle's center.*

11. To remove depression and cavity, open wax around wick by poking a hole down into the center of the candle with a probe, making certain not to poke clear through to the bottom of the mold.

Step 11

12. Using a funnel, carefully refill cavity area with remaining wax to the original level of the candle. Repeat opening and filling process until wax no longer shrinks. *Note: The temperature of the refilling wax is very important. The wax will not adhere to the candle if it is too cool. If the wax is too hot, it may melt through the thin, top edge and spill over in-between the candle and mold. Therefore, make certain the wax is heated to its original temperature.*

Step 12

13. The candle will pull away from the sides of the mold as it cools. When it is completely cold to the touch, remove the seal and pin. Tap or gently squeeze the mold to release the candle. Grasp dowel and

pull candle from the mold. Remove dowel from wick.

Step 13

14. Turn candle upside down so end that was poured into and refilled now becomes the bottom of the candle. Using a sharp knife, slightly dig around wick in bottom of candle. Cut off the wick below the surface.

15. Line a fry pan with aluminum foil. Heat the pan until it is very hot and then turn off the heat.

16. Place the candle in the pan and, holding it straight, quickly rotate it so the bottom becomes flat and even.

Step 16

17. Cut top wick to a ½" length.

18. Carefully trim any seam lines using a sharp knife held at a right angle. Polish seam area with a damp paper towel or gently rub with a nylon stocking.

19. Allow candle to stand at room temperature for at least one hour before burning. For best results, allow candle to stand at room temperature for eight hours.

Rubber Molds
Things Needed
• Things Needed on page 24
• Cardboard
• Liquid detergent
• Masking tape
• Mold collar
• Wicking needle

Instructions
1. Clean and dry mold and then coat with a few drops of liquid detergent.

2. Suspend mold in the mold collar. If a mold collar was not provided, use a heavy piece of cardboard and cut an opening that is slightly smaller than diameter of the lip of the mold.

3. Thread primed wick through the wicking needle. Poke needle through the center top of the mold and up through to base of the mold. Cover hole with mold seal. Pull wick taut without stretching it, and firmly wrap it around the dowel. Lay dowel across bottom of mold, making certain wick is centered.

4. Rest mold collar on top of water bath container.

5. Determine amount of wax needed for mold and melt wax following instructions for Melting Wax on pages 19-21.

6. Follow steps 7-12 for Molded Candles on page 25, for filling, refilling, and cooling in a water bath. Make certain water does not get on candle.

7. When wax has completely hardened, unwind wick from dowel, remove mold collar,

and carefully roll mold off candle the same way a sock is rolled off a foot.

8. Trim both ends of wick and level candle, following steps 14-19 for Molded Candles on page 26.

Two-Piece Molds
Things Needed
• Things Needed on page 24
• Masking tape

Instructions
1. Make certain one section of the mold has an opening for pouring. If it does not, use a sharp knife or scissors to cut an opening in the bottom of the section that does not have the wick groove.

2. Follow manufacturer's instructions for assembling the mold. Lay wick into wick groove and secure it at top and bottom of mold with masking tape. The mold may snap or clamp together. Tape edges together, if necessary, to prevent any seepage and to insure mold is watertight.

3. Place mold in stand. If a stand was not provided, stick mold into a piece of styrofoam or a box of sand to hold it upright.

4. Determine amount of wax needed for mold and melt wax following instructions for Melting Wax on pages 19-21.

5. Follow instructions for Molded Candles on page 24 for filling, refilling, and cooling in a water bath. When wax has completely hardened, carefully separate both sections of mold to release candle.

6. Follow steps 15-17 for Molded Candles on page 25, for trimming seams and leveling the candle.

Finished Molded Candles

Dipped Candles

Create various tapers in different sizes by dipping wicks into melted wax and hanging them to dry. The creation of two or three candles at a time is easily possible.

Things Needed
- Things Needed for Melting Wax on pages 19-21
- Hanger or long nail
- Paring knife
- Tall can
- Wick: flat, primed

Things Needed

Instructions
1. Determine amount of wax needed and melt wax to 160°F following instructions for Melting Wax on pages 19-21. The amount of wax needed depends upon size of the dipping can, and size of the dipping can depends upon the desired height of the candle. As a general guideline, a 12" high by 5¼"-wide can requires 6½ lbs. of cold wax.

2. Cut wick the desired length of the finished candle plus 2". For example, a 6" candle requires 8" of wick.

3. Hold wick at one end and dip end into the wax for three seconds. Remove wick. Hang to cool for three minutes. After 3-4 dippings, straighten wick and candle.

4. Repeat dipping and drying process until candle is the desired thickness. The process may take as many as 15-30 dips. Use an even and smooth motion to dip.

Step 3

Step 4

5. Several times during the dipping process, trim the drips off the bottom of the candle with paring knife.

Step 5

Finished Dipped Candles

6. Heat wax to 180°F for the final dipping to give candle a smooth finish. While still slightly warm, trim the drip off the bottom of candle and gently press bottom against a smooth, hard surface to flatten.

Option: Rather than heating the wax to 180°F for the final dipping, gently roll the cooled candle on wax paper to remove any minor bumps and to give the candle a smooth finish.

7. Hang candle from hanger or nail to dry for at least one hour. Trim wick to ½" length before burning.

Tips for Dipped Candles

▪ For successful dipping, the correct temperature for the melted wax is very important. Dipping in a higher temperature (175°F-180°F) may cause previous layers to melt. Dipping in a low temperature causes the wax layers to adhere unevenly and water may become trapped between the layers.

▪ If desired, color of wax may be deepened at any time during the dipping process by adding more dye to the molten wax. Make certain after adding dye that the wax is still the correct temperature.

▪ If desired, colored layers can be created. Two dips make a narrow band, six dips make a medium-wide band, and ten dips make a wide band.

▪ If the candle is dipped too often or left in the wax too long, it will begin to melt, rather than build up.

Carved Candles

Carved candles are dipped or molded candles that have been carved into a design. This book shows three methods out of many to carve a candle. To carve a molded candle, begin carving immediately after candle is removed from mold.

Simple Carving is when cuts made with a knife blade are nearly parallel to the surface of the candle and remove a shallow section to expose a wide area of the colored dipped coatings. The sections cut out may be discarded or pressed back onto a different area of the candle's surface.

Curl Carving begins by marking flutes in the candle with the edge of a paring knife. This acts as a guide for the start of each cut as shown in Diagram A. The first mark should be approximately 4½" up the side of the candle with the second and each succeeding mark ¾-1" apart.

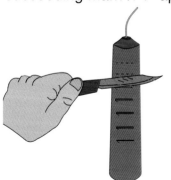

Diagram A

30

If the candle is to be curled all the way to the top, make certain to mark the flutes.

Once the candle is marked, hold the knife nearly vertical but horizontal to the candle. Cut straight down, inclining the cut just slightly toward the center of the candle as shown in Diagram B.

Diagram B

At end of cut, approximately 1" from bottom, the knife should be approximately ³⁄₁₆" in from the surface. Slide knife up and out of cut and pull cut wax slightly away from body of candle to make it easier to grasp. Take tip of cut and roll into a curl as shown in Diagram C. Repeat process around entire bottom row, remembering to work quickly.

Diagram C

Begin second row, stopping approximately ½" above the first row. Try to make each curl consistent with previous curls. For a tapered appearance, make each cut slightly shallower.

Twist Carving follows the basic instructions for Curl Carving, but the cuts are twisted instead of rolled. Pull the cut away from the candle, grasp with fingers, and slide fingers up the curl and twist 180° in a smooth, uniform motion. Lay the tip back against the surface of the candle where the cut originated. A shallow, more parallel cut, not exceeding ⅛", makes a more delicate twist and is easier to handle.

Carved Candles Things Needed
- Things Needed for Melting Wax on pages 19-21
- Things Needed for Dipped Candles on page 28
- Clothes hanger: metal
- Container for additional color

Instructions
1. Following instructions for Melting Wax on pages 19-21, determine amount of wax needed for two containers. Use only one color per container. Melt wax and create two different colors. *Note: If more than two colors*

are desired, determine amount of wax needed for desired number of containers.

2. Make a dipped candle following steps 1-3 for Dipped Candles on page 28. Hang to dry.

3. Dip candle in water in a continuous motion for 45 seconds to cool and so the wax adheres well. Make certain no water is left on the candle. Wipe any remaining water drops off with palm of hand.

4. Continue dipping process in darker colored wax 5-10 more times.

Step 4

5. Begin dipping in lighter colored wax 20-25 times.

Step 5

6. Dip in darker colored wax ten times and then in the lighter colored wax two times.

Freeform Carved Candles

7. Either place candle on a turntable at eye level or hang the candle from a sturdy metal clothes hanger at eye level. Immediately carve candle as desired while it is still hot.

Step 7

Finished Carved Candles

Twisted Candles

Twisted candles are dipped candles that have been shaped into a spiral design. Creating a perfect twisted candle may require practice.

Things Needed
- Things Needed for Melting Wax on pages 19-21
- Things Needed for Dipped Candles on page 28
- Paring knife
- Rolling Pin
- Tall can
- Waxed paper

Instructions
1. Determine amount of wax needed and melt wax following instructions for Melting Wax on pages 19-21.

2. Make dipped candle following instructions for Dipped Candles on pages 28-29.

3. When candle has cooled to the point where it is slightly warm to hold but still pliable, place it on a clean, smooth surface covered with waxed paper and flatten it with a rolling pin to a ¼" thickness. Roll center only, not tip or base.

Step 3

4. Hold candle near wick with one hand and at base with other hand. Keep one hand still and gently twist other hand in an even motion. Continue twisting until entire length is twisted. Work quickly, but not too vigorously, while wax is still warm.

Finished Twisted Candles

Step 4

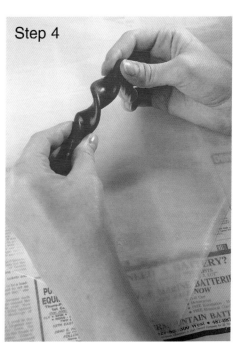

5. If necessary, reshape base of candle to fit into candle holder.

6. Allow candle to cool for at least one hour before burning.

Intricate Twisted Candles

Braided Candles

Braided candles can be created easily with a variation of sizes and colors of taper candles.

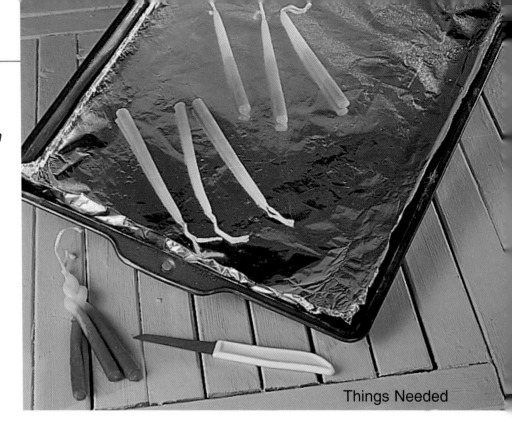

Things Needed

Things Needed
- Aluminum foil
- Cookie sheet
- Extra set of hands
- Oven
- Paring knife
- Taper candles (2-3)

Instructions
1. Gather someone to help and at least two or three taper candles that are the same size.

2. Heat oven to 200°F.

3. Lay taper candles on a cookie sheet and place in oven to soften candles. Check frequently to make certain candles have not melted.

4. Have someone hold the base of the candles, tips pointing down. Braid candles, working quickly while the candles are soft, and making certain all the wicks come together at the same point.

Step 4

5. Gently twist and mold the tips and bases together to form one candle. If unable to completely twist the bases together, twist as far as possible and cut remaining ends off.

Finished Braided Candles

33

Beeswax Rolled Candles

Beoswax rolled candles are created with thin sheets of beeswax. These candles can take on several forms. They offer a delicious, yet natural scent.

Things Needed
- Blow dryer
- Craft knife
- Metal-edge ruler
- Scissors: craft
- Sheet of beeswax: rectangular
- Wick: square, primed

Instructions

1. Warm rectangular piece of beeswax with a blow dryer so it becomes soft and pliable. The short side of the rectangle determines the height of the candle.

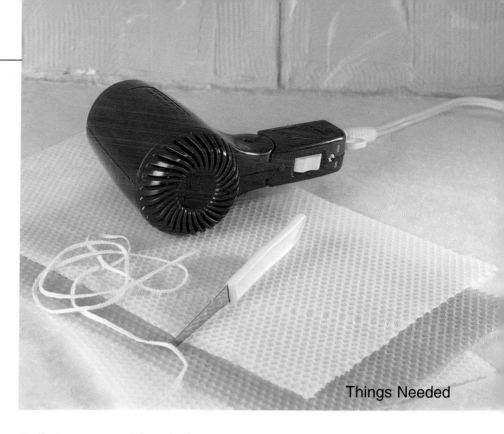

Things Needed

2. Cut a narrow triangle from the longest side of the rectangle using a ruler and craft knife.

3. Cut wick ¾" longer than height of the candle. Gently press wick into longest short edge and begin rolling, making certain wick is firmly in place after the first roll.

Step 1

Step 2

Step 3

4. Roll candle. The tighter the candle is rolled, the longer it will burn.

Step 4

5. When rolling is complete, press the edge into the candle. Beeswax is sticky so it will adhere to itself.

Step 5

6. Trim wick to a ½" length.

7. If powdery residue forms on wax either after making or during storage, remove by blowing candle with blow dryer.

Rolled Straight Beeswax

1. Warm rectangular piece of beeswax with a blow dryer so it becomes soft and pliable. The short side of the rectangle determines the height of the candle.

2. Either leave the beeswax sheet as it is for a single, tall candle or cut it in half for two smaller candles.

3. Follow steps 3-7 for Beeswax Rolled Candles on pages 34-35.

Spiral Beeswax Taper

1. Warm rectangular piece of beeswax with blow dryer so it becomes soft and pliable.

2. Cut rectangular piece in half diagonally from top corner to bottom corner.

3. Follow steps 3-7 for Beeswax Rolled Candles on page 34-35.

Two-Toned Spiral Beeswax Taper

1. Follow the instructions for a Spiral Taper Beeswax Candles above, except use two different colors of beeswax.

2. Slightly offset and overlap the two different colored rectangles.

Sandwiching Beeswax Shapes

1. Warm a rectangular piece of beeswax with a blow dryer so it becomes soft and pliable.

2. Cut wick ¾" longer than the desired height of candle. Cut beeswax into an equal number of desired shapes such as squares or stars. See Diagram A.

Diagram A

3. Sandwich wick between two pieces of beeswax. See Diagram B.

Diagram B

4. Continue sandwiching the pieces of wax, applying equal pressure as the candle is built outward. See Diagram C on page 36. For a three-dimensional appearance,

gradually decrease size of each layer.

Diagram C

5. Trim wick to a ½" length.

Tips for Beeswax Candles

■ Beeswax works best if dipped or rolled because of its sticky texture.

■ Beeswax can be purchased in several different colors.

■ Beeswax candles can be molded, however, a special release agent should be placed inside the mold.

■ Beeswax candles and ornaments tend to develop a powdery residue when stored. Remove by blowing candle or ornament with a blow dryer. See photo below.

Finished Beeswax Candles

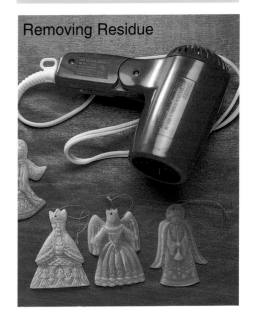

Removing Residue

Whipped Candles

Whipped candles are made using whipped wax. Whipped wax can be used to create theme candles.

Things Needed

Things Needed
- Things Needed for Melting Wax on pages 19-21
- Candle, ice cream cone, or decorative dish
- Container: deep and wide
- Fork; spoon; spatula
- Wire whisk
- Wick: wire core, primed

Instructions
1. Melt wax following instructions for Melting Wax on pages 19-21.

2. Cool wax just to the point where a thin film appears on the surface. Quickly whip wax into a froth using a wire whisk. The faster the wax is whipped, the fluffier it becomes.

Step 2

Tips for Whipped Candles
- After wax has melted, add one tablespoon of cornstarch per pound of wax, and the wax will adhere better to the candle.

- Add one tablespoon of washing detergent per pound of wax at any time during the whipping process for added whiteness.

- Whipped colored wax will be much lighter than when poured.

3. Whipped wax needs to be applied to a candle or placed into desired container immediately before wax hardens. Whipped wax can be applied in three different methods. However, regardless of method chosen, whipped wax should be applied immediately.

3a. Whipped wax can be applied to a candle with a spoon or placed into an ice cream cone or dish. If placing whipped wax into ice cream cone or dish, insert wick before whipped wax dries. See photo on page 38.

Step 3a

3c. Whipped wax can be applied to a candle with a fork.

Step 3c

3d. Whipped wax can be applied to a candle by dipping candle into the whipped wax.

Step 3d

3b. Whipped wax can be applied with a spatula *Note: Clear whipped wax has been added to the candles in steps 3b-3d.*

Step 3b

Finished Whipped Candles

Floating Candles

Floating candles are molded in molds that are wider than they are high. This is what allows them to float. Candy, petit fours, and individual gelatin molds are ideal for floating candles.

Things Needed

- Things Needed for Melting Wax on pages 19-21
- Things Needed for Molded Candles on page 24
- Needles: large-eyed (if using candy molds)
- Mold: wider than height
- Paring knife
- Pliers
- Wick: floating, primed

Instructions

1. Determine amount of wax needed and melt wax following instructions for Melting Wax on pages 19-21.

2. Cut wick 1½" longer than height of the molds. Place one end of the wick into the hole in wick tab and crimp shut with pliers, making certain wick is secure.

3. Clean and dry the mold and then coat with mold release, silicone spray, or vegetable oil. See Wick Tabs on page 13. Place wick tab and wick in center bottom of each mold. Carefully pour wax into the molds to within ½" of the top. Gently tap sides of molds to release any air bubbles.

Step 4

4. Set molds in a pan filled with shallow water to cool. If necessary, weight the molds down to keep them from floating.

5. Follow steps 11-12 on page 25 for Molded Candles. Only one refilling should be necessary, because of the small size of the candles. When refilling, make certain wax is poured over wick to coat it for easier lighting and burning.

6. When wax has completely hardened, remove molds from water bath and turn them over to release the candles from molds. Trim wicks to ½" lengths.

Candy Molds

1. Determine amount of wax needed and melt wax following instructions for Melting Wax on pages 19-21.

2. Clean and dry the molds and then coat with mold release, silicone spray, or vegetable oil. Carefully pour wax into the molds to within ½" of the top. Gently tap sides of molds to release any air bubbles. Let wax cool.

3. Remove candles from molds. Heat a large-eyed needle.

Step 4

39

4. Insert needle through center of molded candles and remove.

5. Put a primed wick into holes. Seal wick hole at bottom of candles with a small drop of wax.

6. Trim candles with a paring knife.

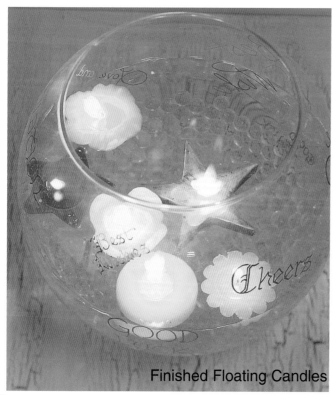

Finished Floating Candles

Tips for Floating Candles

■ Cut wicks short, so flame stays low.

■ Burning a number of floating candles in group of six or more provides a larger amount of light because their light is reflected off the water.

Treasure Candles

Treasure candles are molded with a special trinket(s) inside the wax.

Things Needed
- Things Needed for Melting Wax on pages 19-21
- Things Needed for Molded Candles on page 24
- Charms, coins, or trinkets: anything that will not burn or melt

Instructions
1. Determine amount of wax needed and melt wax following instructions for Melting Wax on pages 19-21.

2. Follow instructions for Molded Candles on pages 24-26. After pouring wax into mold, let it cool for 15-20 minutes in lukewarm water and then add desired treasures.

3. Cool for 30 minutes longer and then add more treasures, if desired. Continue following the instructions to complete a molded candle.

Finished Treasure Candles

Cubed Candles

Cubed candles are molded candles with cubed pieces of wax in them. These unique candles can be bright or elegant depending on the mold and the colors of the cubed pieces.

Things Needed

- Things Needed for Melting Wax on pages 19-21
- Things Needed for Molded Candles on page 24
- Containers: one for each color
- Dyes: as desired
- Ice cube trays
- Wick: wire core, primed

Note: Cubes of colored wax are available at candle making stores or they may be made using ice cube trays and dyes.

Instructions

1. Determine amount of wax needed for ice cube trays and mold and melt wax following instructions for Melting Wax on pages 19-21. Do not add any dye to wax that will be used for the large, molded candle; it needs to be clear.

2. Pour individual colored waxes into clean dry ice cube trays.

3. Cool and remove cubes from trays. Cut into chunks or smaller cubes with paring knife.

Step 3

4. Fill desired mold with cubes. Place wick in center of cubes and then pour clear wax into mold. Follow steps 9-18 for Molded Candles on pages 25-26 to complete candle.

Step 4

Finished Cubed Candles

Pinched Candles

Any candle can be turned into a original pinched candle. The deeper the pinch, the larger the design. Vary angles and spacing using different sizes of tools.

Things Needed

Things Needed
- Candle: as desired
- Forceps
- Pans (2)
- Pliers
- Stove
- Tweezers

Instructions

1. Fill one pan with cold water. Fill other pan with water and heat to 165°F.

2. Dip candle into hot water just long enough to soften surface.

3. Warm pinching tool (forceps, tweezers, or pliers) and immediately pinch wax surface. Work quickly. If wax hardens, dip candle into hot water again.

4. After pinching is completed, dip candle quickly in hot water once more and smooth out any roughness and then dip candle in cold water to set design.

Step 2

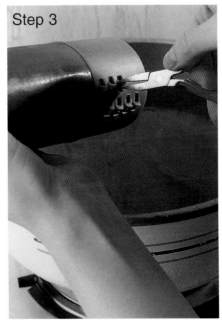
Step 3

Finished Pinched Candles

Double Mold Candles

Double Mold Candles are candles with an outer shell of wax that displays embedded items. After the candle has melted down, the outer shell can be used as hurricane for a votive candle.

Things Needed
- Things Needed for Melting Wax on pages 19-21
- Things Needed for Molded Candles on page 24
- Candle: clear or light colored
- Mold: to fit around desired candle
- Naturals: as desired

Instructions

1. Melt wax following instructions for Melting Wax on pages 19-21. Wax should be clear or a light color to let desired item(s) shine through.

2. Prepare mold using mold release, silicone spray, or vegetable oil. Place purchased or premade candle inside mold with wick facing up. Candle should be level with mold for best results.

3. Add desired naturals to melted wax. Mix. *Option: To only have a few items placed randomly in outer shell, pour melted wax into mold and let it set up, but not completely. Place items into wax as*

44

desired using craft stick. Smooth over any holes with craft stick. Fill in holes with melted wax.

4. Pour melted wax into mold.

5. Use craft stick to spread melted wax and naturals evenly if needed.

Step 5

6. Melted wax should cover the top of the purchased candle, but should not cover wick.

7. Remove mold following steps 9-12 of Molded Candles on page 25.

Ideas for Double Mold Candles
- Cinnamon sticks
- Coins
- Dried beans
- Dried fruit
- Dried flowers
- Dried leaves
- Flat marbles
- Glass pieces
- Metal beads
- Metal charms
- Potpourri
- Pressed flowers
- Rose petals
- Seashells

Finished Double Mold Candles

Sand Candles

Sand candles are simply candles molded in damp sand. The star sand candle below also uses techniques from Double Mold Candles on page 44.

Things Needed
- Things Needed for Melting Wax on pages 19-21
- Things Needed for Mold Candles on page 24
- Bowls: mixing, large; small
- Needles: large-eyed
- Sand: damp
- Spoon: metal

Instructions

1. Fill large mixing bowl or container half full with firmly packed damp sand.

2. Push small bowl into the center of the packed sand. Add more sand and pack around small bowl if necessary. Carefully remove bowl.

3. Measure depth of the hole and add 1" for the length of the wick.

4. Determine amount of wax needed and melt wax following instructions for Melting Wax on pages 19-21.

5. Gently pour wax into center of sand, trickling it over the back of a spoon so it does not cause the sand to lose its shape. The wax will seep into the sand within five minutes.

Step 5

6. Add more wax. After two hours, a well will form in the center and more wax will need to be added.

7. Heat large-eyed needle using heating element. Push large-eyed needle down through center of the well and pull it back out. Place wick into hole and wrap excess around a dowel. Rest dowel across top of sand.

8. Allow candle to cool for three hours and then remove candle from mold. Smooth and shape as desired.

9. Level bottom of candle following steps 15-16 for Molded Candles on page 26. Trim wick to a ½" length.

Finished Sand Candles

Citronella Candles

Citronella candles are made from fragrance oils distilled from a fragrant grass grown in China, Malaysia, Sri Lanka, and Central America. The lemony fragrance is used in soaps, deodorizers, and insecticides. These candles are used to repel mosquitoes.

Citronella candles are made by adding the fragrance during the candle making process. A variety of containers such as small pails and pottery are ideal for use as molds.

The wick of a citronella candle is typically larger to increase wax melting. The larger the pool of molten wax, the greater the fragrance and effectiveness.

For best results, space candles every 5-10 feet. If the weather is hot, moist, or windy, increase the number of candles. Place candles outdoors one hour before sunset. Candles are not effective until a pool of molten wax forms. Keep candles lit as long as people remain outdoors.

Citronella candles repel as many as 25,000 varieties of mosquitoes and are effective against some other small, flying insects. Some insects such as moths, however, are attracted to the light of the flame.

Citronella Candles

Aromatherapy Candles

These candles use essential oils to help balance the human body and work in harmony with nature. The oils can be added into the melted wax or added to a purchased unscented candle.

Things Needed
- Things Needed for Melting Wax on pages 19-21
- Dropper
- Essential oil: as desired
- Wick: square, primed

Instructions
1. See Melting Wax on pages 19-21. Melt wax. Add color if desired.

2. Add 2-3 drops of essential oil to melted wax.

3. Make desired candle in this chapter.

Purchased Candle
Things Needed
- Candle: unscented
- Essential oil: as desired
- Metal ice pick

Instructions
1. For thin candles, place several drops of oil on wax before lighting the candle. Avoid dripping oil into flame or on wick. For thick candles, heat a metal ice pick over heating element. Pierce two holes close to the wick. Insert pick ½ of the way into the candle. Turn candle upside down and shake out any lose wax.

2. Add essential oils. Holes will appear less noticeable after the candle has been burned.

Step 2

Aromatic Effects
- Clove relieves pain, uplifts mood, helps relieve fatigue, and improves digestion.

- Eucalyptus relieves pain, breaks up congestion, reduces inflammation.

- Grapefruit uplifts mood, energizes, and increases physical strength.

- Jasmine uplifts mood and is an aphrodisiac.

- Lemon calms, balances nervous system, and improves digestion.

- Orange calms and reduces stress.

- Pine lessens pain, energizes, and helps breathing.

Finished Aromatherapy Candles

47

Tallow Candles

Tallow candles are made from beef or mutton fat. Tallow candles smell like grease and are used for light, not decorative or fragrant purposes. Tallow is most commonly dipped, but it can also be made into a molded candle.

Things Needed
- Beef or mutton fat: 5-10 lbs.
- Bowl: mixing, large
- Cheese cloth
- Hanger or long nail
- Knife
- Plastic wrap
- Spoon: slotted
- Stock pot or canning pot
- Wick: flat

Instructions
1. Gather a large stock or canning pot, 5-10 lbs. of mutton or beef fat, slotted spoon or sieve, cheesecloth, and a large mixing bowl for rendering the tallow.

2. Rinse fat with cool water and trim all meat scraps off. Chop fat into thumb-size pieces. The smaller the pieces, the better it will render.

3. Fill a large pot ⅓-½ full of fat pieces. Add water to within 1" of the top of the pot. Heat to a low boil for two hours, stirring every 15-20 minutes and skimming off any foam or residue from top. Add more water as it boils down, being careful of possible sputtering.

4. Take pot off heat and remove cracklings (little gray, shrunken pieces of fat) with a slotted spoon or sieve. Carefully strain remaining liquid through several layers of cheesecloth into a large mixing bowl. Allow liquid to cool for several hours and then place bowl in refrigerator to chill.

5. As liquid cools, tallow rises to the top and solidifies. Remove tallow from bowl and discard remaining liquid. If a gelatin-like substance has formed on bottom of tallow, simply scrape it off and discard.

Note: If tallow is fully rendered, it will be firm, uniform in color, and smooth in texture. If, at room temperature, it is yellowish, soft, grainy, or oily looking, put it in a pot with an equal amount of water. Bring it to a boil, strain it into a bowl, and let it cool. Repeat as necessary until all impurities are removed.

6. Wrap finished block of tallow in plastic wrap and store it in the refrigerator for up to two months.

7. Make dipped tallow candle following instructions for Dipped Candles on page 28.

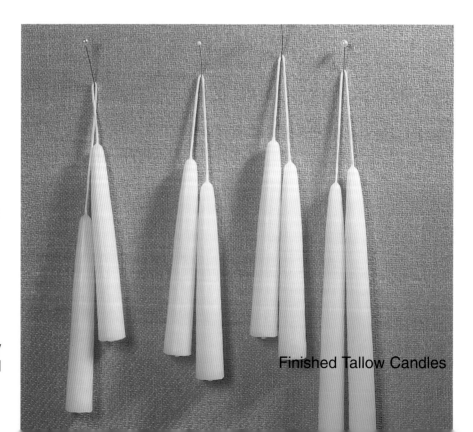
Finished Tallow Candles

Chapter Five:

Holiday & Celebration Candles

Egg Tower Candle

Things Needed

- Bead wax
- Egg dyes: commercial
- Eggs: raw (13)
- Glue gun and glue sticks
- Paper towels
- Wicks: wire core, primed

Instructions

1. Following commercial egg dye manufacturer's instructions, dye raw eggs for a brief amount of time to obtain pastel colors.

2. Crack a small hole in the top of each egg and, using fingers, remove top third of shell. Pour egg white and yolk out and carefully clean egg shell under running water. Pat eggs dry with paper towels.

3. Using glue gun, glue five eggs together at sides to form a circle. Glue four eggs on top of five egg circle. Create a third layer with three eggs and finish with one egg at top. When gluing egg layers, make certain each egg points toward outside of circle slightly before gluing. After glue is in place, positioning is impossible.

4. Fill each egg shell with bead wax and insert wick into the top egg shell only.

Dessert Candles

Things Needed
- Things Needed for Whipped Candles on page 37
- Aluminum foil
- Candy sprinkles
- Cooking spray: non-stick
- Cup: disposable plastic
- Cup cake papers
- Dyes: green; red; yellow
- Ice cream cones
- Ice cream shake glass
- Needles: large-eyed
- Scissors: craft
- Spoon: plastic
- Straw: drinking, bendable
- Sundae dish
- Vegetable peeler
- Wick tab
- Wicks: square, primed; wire core, primed

Instructions
See Whipped Candles on pages 37-38 to prepare whipped wax. If whipped wax hardens up too much during sculpting process, it can be returned to double boiler to repeat the process.

Hot Fudge Sundae
1. Fill sundae dish to the top with whipped wax. While the wax is still soft, insert wire core wick into center. The wax should be soft enough to insert the wick, but hard enough to keep the wick in place.

2. Once wick is in place, allow wax to cool completely.

The candle can be placed into the freezer to speed up the process.

3. When candle has cooled, build up more whipped wax on top of the cooled wax and around the wick using a plastic spoon. As wax is built up, form "scoop" indentations in it to make the wax look like hand-scooped ice cream. When desired look is achieved, allow wax to cool completely.

Chocolate Sauce
1. See Melting Wax on pages 19-21. Melt 1½" cube of wax in double boiler. Add two squares each of green and red candle dye to produce a deep reddish brown wax.

2. Once mixture has melted completely, spoon or pour it over the cooled whipped wax. Allow poured wax to cool completely before touching it, or fingerprints will be left.

Cherries
1. See Melting Wax on pages 19-21. Melt a 2-3" cube of wax in double boiler. Add one or two squares red candle dye (depending on depth of color desired in cherries).

2. When mixture has melted completely, let it cool slightly and then pour it out onto a

piece of aluminum foil. While wax is still malleable, but not liquid, cut or tear wax into strips and roll it between hands to form ball the size of a cherry.

3. Use large-eyed needle to puncture a small hole in cherry for the wick to go through. Thread cherry onto wick and press it slightly into surrounding wax. The cherry can be fused to wax by carefully running a flame or hot air over it. This will also remove fingerprints and blemishes. Make certain not to heat too much, or the wax will melt and run.

4. Once cherry has cooled, wick can be trimmed down to desired length.

Ice Cream Cones
1. See Melting Wax on pages 19-21. Seal ice cream cone by dipping it for a few seconds in melted wax. Hold it upside down to let excess wax drip off.

2. Once it has cooled, add whipped wax and wick to cone as in Hot Fudge Sundae instructions.

Chocolate Shake
1. Fill an ice cream shake glass to the rim with reddish-brown whipped wax colored with two squares each of

green and red dye. Insert wire wick into center. Allow to cool completely.

2. Top with white whipped wax, fluffed up to look like whipping cream. Before white wax cools completely, insert half of a bendable straw into the side. Cover with chocolate sprinkles formed by shaving cooled or malleable chocolate sauce colored wax with a vegetable peeler. Trim wick to desired length.

Cupcakes

1. See Melting Wax on pages 19-21. Melt wax.

2. Using craft scissors, cut top half off of a disposable plastic cup. Spray inside of bottom half lightly with non-stick cooking spray. Set aside. Dip cupcake paper into clear melted wax for a few seconds then put it in the bottom of the plastic cup to harden.

3. See Wick Tabs on page 13. Place square wick and wick tab into bottom center of cupcake paper. Pour melted wax into cupcake paper. Allow candle to cool completely. Remove from plastic cup.

4. See Whipped Candles on pages 37-38.

5. Build up pink whipped wax on top and around wick to look like frosting. Before it cools, thread wax cherry onto wick and press it slightly into the soft pink wax. Press real candy sprinkles into whipped wax around top of candle, staying clear of wick. Trim wick to desired length.

Stamped Halloween Candle

Things Needed
• Embossing powder: clear
• Glue: craft
• Heat gun
• Measuring tape
• Paper: heavy-weight, black
• Pigment stamping ink: silver
• Pillar candle
• Scissors: craft
• Stamps: halloween theme
• Straight pins

Instructions
1. Measure circumference of candle to determine length of paper needed for wrap. Mark measurement on black heavy-weight paper. Width of paper will be determined by height of stamped scene.

2. Using silver pigment ink, stamp a scene across paper with halloween theme stamps.

3. Sprinkle each stamped design with clear embossing powder and set with heat gun.

4. Using craft scissors, cut stamped scene out leaving a small border of black around stamped designs.

5. Stamped scene can be secured in place temporarily with straight pins pushed through back seam of paper into candle. Or for permanent attachment, stamped scene can be glued in place with craft glue.

Make a candle for each holiday. For example, use a white pillar candle, green pigment stamping ink, and a Christmas tree stamp to create a Christmas decoration.

Make a candle as a gift, rubber stamp someone's initials on the candle. Give it to him/her as a gift.

Mug Candles

Things Needed
- Bead wax
- Colored pencils: as desired
- Glue: découpage
- Mugs: glass, beer (4)
- Paintbrush: flat
- Scissors: craft
- Spoon

Instructions

1. Photocopy Labels A-D on pages 55-56 at copy center. Labels can be colored in with colored pencils. Using craft scissors, cut out each label.

2. Using découpage glue and flat paintbrush, spread découpage glue on back of labels. Adhere labels to center of beer mugs. See photo on page 54.

3. Using spoon, insert bead wax into mugs.

Candles can be poured into mugs using a wick, wick tab, and melted wax. See Melting Wax on pages 19-21. Make certain mug is warm to prevent cracking. Warm mug with a blow dryer or heat in oven.

Label A   Actual size

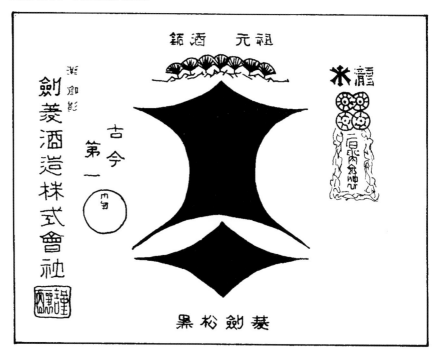

Label B   Actual size

Label C   Actual size

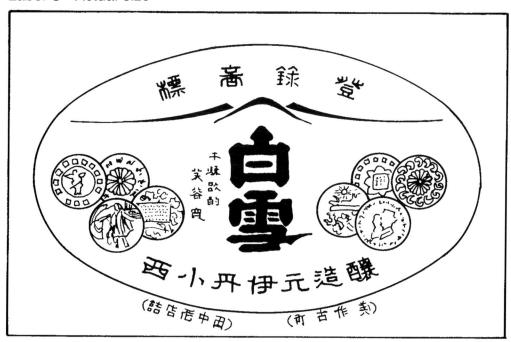

Label D   Actual size

Découpage Candles

Photos on pages 57-58.

Things Needed

- Blow dryer
- Craft knife
- Decorative tissue paper or paper napkin: as desired
- Glue: découpage
- Paintbrush: flat
- Pillar candle
- Polyurethane
- Scissors: craft

Instructions

1. Using craft scissors, cut tissue paper or napkin ½" larger than candle in both circumference and length.

2. Using flat paintbrush, spread découpage glue on candle in a 1½" vertical strip. Lay tissue paper down on a flat surface. Lay glued area of candle down on paper, keeping candle straight and centered. Add more glue to candle a little at a time and roll candle onto paper to adhere. Continue until candle sides are completely covered. Use fingers to smooth out wrinkles or bubbles. Some wrinkles will remain. Allow to dry.

3. Using craft knife, trim excess paper carefully at top and bottom.

4. Apply 5-10 coats of polyurethane over candle sides, allowing each coat to dry completely before adding next. A blow dryer can be used to speed up drying process.

Candle wax can be used for more than candles. Try making a wax seal on a journal.

Candle Wax Seal

Things Needed
- Acrylic paints: gold; another color of choice
- Charm: brass filigree
- Glue: craft
- Ice cubes
- Journal: small, blank
- Matches
- Metal monogram seal
- Paper towels
- Ribbons: as desired
- Scissors: fabric
- Sponge
- Taper candle: with color

throughout candle, not just on outside

Instructions
1. With sponge and acrylic paint, lightly sponge paint on cover of journal.

2. Wrap front journal cover with a variety of ribbons, glue each in place to inside of book cover or to front of book cover. Visible ribbon ends can be cut in dovetails with craft scissors. Loop one ribbon and glue it to front of book. Glue brass charm over looped ribbon.

3. Place metal seal on an ice cube to cool. Light candle and let it burn long enough to drip about 15 drops of wax onto center of brass charm. Wipe moisture off seal using a paper towel and press into puddle of wax. Let seal rest on surface of wax for a few seconds and then lift.

4. When wax impression has cooled completely, using fingertips, apply a touch of gold paint to raised areas of wax.

Note: Since the modern postal service is automated, seals on envelopes that will be mailed are not recommended.

59

Chapter Six:
Decorating Candles

Gold Indented Votive

Things Needed
• Acrylic paint: metallic gold
• Electric stove burner
• Paintbrush: flat
• Paper plate
• Phillips head screwdriver
• Votive candle

Instructions
1. Turn stove burner on high and wait for it to heat up. Lay tip of screwdriver on burner, rotating screwdriver to heat evenly.

2. Hold candle in one hand over paper plate. Holding candle above heated screwdriver, push heated tip into candle making ¼"-deep impressions. Allow melted candle wax to drip onto paper plate, not back onto candle.

3. Using metallic gold paint, paint candle.

Gold Studded Votive

Things Needed
• Craft nail heads (commonly used to decorate T-shirts)
• Votive candle

Instructions
1. Practice design placement of nail heads on a flat surface before attaching them to the candle.

2. Push nail heads into candle in desired placement design.

Gold Swirl Votive

Things Needed
• Marker: metallic gold, medium-point
• Paper: scrap
• Votive candle

Instructions
1. Using metallic gold marker, practice desired design on a scrap piece of paper before drawing on candle.

2. Draw design onto candle. Go over markings two or three times to make a thicker, solid line.

Gold Leaf Votive

Things Needed
• Glue gun and glue sticks: low temperature
• Gold leafing adhesive
• Gold leafing
• Paintbrushes: flat; liner
• Votive candle

Instructions
1. Using a low temperature glue gun, apply glue streams in a design on candle as desired or using photograph for placement.

2. Using gold leaf adhesive and liner brush, paint over raised glue design area. Allow adhesive to sit at least 30 minutes. Apply gold leafing to adhesive on raised glue design. Use a flat paintbrush to brush off excess gold leafing.

Gold Stamped Votive

Things Needed
• Acrylic paint: metallic gold
• Paper plate
• Stamp: miniature
• Votive candle

Instructions
1. Pour a small amount of acrylic paint into paper plate. Spread paint out in an even layer.

2. Dip stamp into paint and carefully stamp candle, dipping in paint again with each stamp.

Gold Trim Votive

Things Needed
• Acrylic paint: metallic gold
• Paintbrush: liner
• Paper: scrap
• Votive candle

Instructions
1. Pour a small amount of acrylic paint into paper plate. Spread paint out in an even layer.

2. Using liner paintbrush, paint bottom half of candle in swirls or squiggles as desired.

Crackle Candle
Things Needed
- Acrylic gesso
- Acrylic paint: off-white
- Antiquing medium
- Charms: as desired
- Paintbrush: flat
- Pillar candle
- Rag
- Silicone: clear
- Tea light candle
- Two step mosaic crackle medium and activator

Instructions
1. Using clear silicone, adhere charms onto candle. Allow to dry overnight.

2. Using flat paintbrush, apply acrylic gesso over sides of pillar candle and charms. Several coats may be necessary to provide full coverage. Make certain no acrylic gesso gets on top of candle where burning occurs.

3. Mix off-white acrylic paint with first step of mosaic crackle medium. Following manufacturer's instructions, determine ratio of paint to medium. Paint mixture onto candle sides. Allow to set for 30 minutes.

4. Paint over candle sides with mosaic crackle activator. If working area is cool, cracking may take more time.

5. Using a rag, rub antiquing medium over candle sides.

6. Burn candle down just enough to place a tea light candle in top for burning.

Wire Patina Candle
Things Needed
- Fiber mâché
- Glue: industrial-strength
- Paintbrush: flat
- Paper towels
- Patina reactive metallic paint
- Patina aging solution
- Pillar candle
- Polyurethane
- Straight pins
- Tea light candle
- Wire mesh

Instructions
1. Cover sides of candle with wire mesh. Secure in back with industrial-strength glue. Use straight pins to hold mesh in place until glue is dry.

2. Paint sides of pillar candle with patina reactive metallic paint. Allow paint to dry. Apply another coat of metallic paint. While the paint is still wet, apply patina aging solution to sides. Allow to dry two hours. A paper towel can be used to wipe excess paint from candle.

3. Sprinkle fiber mâché over slightly damp candle. Use flat paintbrush to brush off excess. Allow candle to dry completely.

4. Apply one coat of polyurethane over sides of candle.

5. Burn candle down just enough to place a tea light candle in top for burning.

Faux Candle
Things Needed
- Acrylic gesso
- Faux finish: packaged
- Paintbrushes: flat
- Pillar candle
- Tea light candle

Instructions
1. Using flat paintbrush, apply acrylic gesso over sides of pillar candle. Several coats may be necessary to provide full coverage. Make certain no acrylic gesso gets on top of candle where burning occurs.

2. Following manufacturer's instructions, apply faux finish to candle sides.

3. Burn candle down just enough to place a tea light candle in top for burning.

Checkered Cube
Things Needed
- Blow dryer
- Craft knife
- Glue: découpage
- Paintbrush: flat
- Paper or stationery: as desired
- Polyurethane
- Scissors: craft
- Square candle
- Tea light candle

Instructions
1. Using craft scissors, cut paper to cover top and sides of square candle. Cut 1½" circle in center of top paper.

2. Using flat paintbrush, spread découpage glue onto candle. Place paper onto glue. Continue until entire candle is covered. Use fingers to smooth out wrinkles or bubbles. Some bubbles will remain. Allow to dry.

3. Using craft knife, trim excess paper at top.

4. Apply 5-10 coats of polyurethane over candle sides, allowing each coat to dry completely before adding next. A blow dryer can be used to speed up drying process.

5. Burn candle down just enough to place a tea light candle in top for burning.

Celestial Square
Things Needed
- Acrylic paint: navy blue
- Beads
- Blow dryer
- Charms: celestial
- Glue: craft
- Paintbrush: flat
- Paper: heavy, 1½" circle
- Paper towels
- Polyurethane
- Rhinestones
- Spray paint: metallic gold
- Square candle
- Tea light candle
- Wire cutters

Instructions
1. Using wire cutters, cut off loops of charms. Using craft glue, attach charms, beads, and rhinestones to sides of candle as desired. Allow glue to dry completely.

2. Place 1½" circle of heavy paper over wick on candle to keep paint off. Spray candle and charms with metallic gold spray paint, covering completely. Working in a small area at a time, brush over candle and charms with diluted navy blue acrylic paint using a flat paintbrush. Get paint into all crevices and then immed-iately dab wet paint with a crumpled paper towel. Paint should be blotchy looking.

3. Apply 5-10 coats of polyurethane over candle sides, allowing each coat to dry completely before adding next. A blow dryer can be used to speed up drying process. Remove paper circle over wick.

4. Burn candle down just enough to place a tea light candle in top for burning.

Seed Candle
Photo on page 66.
Things Needed
- Glue: craft
- Seeds: celery; hollyhock; mustard; watermelon; zucchini
- Paper plate
- Pillar candle

Instructions
1. Pour mustard seeds onto a paper plate. Using fingertips, rub craft glue on bottom two-thirds of candle. Roll candle in mustard seeds.

2. Pour celery seeds onto candle and push into candle between mustard seeds.

3. To make flowers, use zucchini seeds for petals, hollyhock seeds for centers, and watermelon seeds for leaves. Glue each in place.

flowers to candle as desired. Attach leaves around candle. Repeat with leaves.

2. Tie raffia around candle.

Twig Candle
Things Needed
- Glue gun and glue sticks: low temperature
- Pillar candle
- Raffia
- Scissors: craft
- Twigs

Instructions
1. Using craft scissors, cut twigs to desired size using craft scissors. Using low temperature glue gun, attach twigs to candle as desired.

2. Tie raffia around candle.

Flowers & Leaves
Things Needed
- Dried flowers: as desired
- Dried leaves: as desired
- Glue gun and glue sticks: low temperature
- Pillar candle
- Raffia
- Scissors: craft

Instructions
1. Using craft scissors, cut dried flowers to desired length. Using low temperature glue gun, attach

Make a candle for a favorite teacher by decorating it with different lengths of crayons or colored pencils. Tie with school motif ribbon.

Painted Tapers
Things Needed
- Acrylic paints: as desired
- Aluminum foil
- Paintbrushes: round
- Taper candles (2)
- Toothbrush: old

Instructions
1. Squeeze quarter size amount of each paint onto aluminum foil.

2. Hold candle by the bottom. Paint candle using one of two methods:

Dab paintbrush into paint and allow to drip onto candle. Repeat with other colors until desired look is achieved.

Or spatter by dipping bristles of toothbrush into paint that has been slightly diluted with water. Hold toothbrush about 6–8" away with bristles pointing toward the candle. Draw finger or thumb across bristles causing paint to spatter onto the candle. Repeat with other colors until desired look is achieved.

3. Place on clean piece of aluminum foil to dry or hang if using double tapers.

Billiard Ball Candles
Things Needed
- Acrylic paints: black; blue; green; maroon; orange; purple; red; yellow
- Cardboard: lightweight, 2" square
- Candle spray: gloss finish
- Craft knife
- Paintbrushes: flat; liner
- Pencil
- Round candles: white (16)

Instructions
1. Prepare pattern by drawing a 1"-diameter circle onto lightweight cardboard. Using craft knife, cut out circle with craft knife. Discard center piece of pattern. Place pattern at top of candle about ½" below wick. Using pencil, trace around hole in pattern making a slight indentation in candle. Repeat with all except one candle to be left plain for cue ball.

2. To make solid pool balls, leaving circle below wick blank, use flat paintbrush to paint one candle with each of the following colors of acrylic paint: yellow, blue, red, purple, orange, green, maroon, and black.

3. To make striped balls, use liner paintbrush to paint a ⅛"-thick line around circle beneath wick using one of the

Use melted wax to seal bottles for a decorative look and airtight seal.

Sealed Bottles
Things Needed
- Things Needed for Melting Wax on pages 19-21
- Bottle
- Contents to fill bottle: as desired
- Cork

Instructions
1. Fill bottle with desired contents.

2. Press cork firmly into top of bottle. A small part of cork top should remain outside bottle.

3. See Melting Wax on pages 19-21. Holding bottle upside down, dip it into melted wax. Continue dipping, building up wax to desired level.

following colors on each ball: yellow, blue, red, purple, orange, green, and maroon. Approximately 1" below circle, paint a 1¼"-wide stripe around each striped ball in the same color.

4. Using liner paintbrush, paint numbers in circles on balls as follows:

#1 solid yellow
#2 solid blue
#3 solid red
#4 solid purple
#5 solid orange
#6 solid green
#7 solid maroon
#8 solid black
#9 striped yellow
#10 striped blue
#11 striped red
#12 striped purple
#13 striped orange
#14 striped green
#15 striped maroon

5. Spray candles with gloss finish for added shine.

Stenciled Candle

Things Needed
- Acrylic paints: green; ivory; lt. blue; 3-4 other colors as desired
- Glue: découpage, gloss finish
- Glue gun and glue sticks: low temperature
- Masking tape
- Paintbrush: flat
- Pillar candle
- Sandpaper
- Spanish moss
- Spray paint: blue; white
- Spray sealer: matte; gloss
- Stencils: ivy, small; topiary, small
- Stenciling brush
- Tea light candle
- Terra-cotta flowerpot dish

Instructions
1. Cover wick with masking tape. Spray paint candle with 2-4 coats of blue spray paint. Allow to dry between coats. Lightly spray white spray paint in random cloud like patterns on candle.

2. Apply two coats of matte spray sealer.

3. Stencil candle using 3-4 colors of acrylic paint.

4. Using flat paintbrush, spread a thin coat of gloss découpage glue to entire candle. Spray candle with gloss spray sealer.

5. Wash terra-cotta flowerpot dish with green, lt. blue, and ivory acrylic paint. Allow some of the terra-cotta color to show through. When paint has dried, lightly sand edges of dish to distress.

6. Place pillar candle in center of dish. Using a glue gun, secure Spanish moss to rim of dish and around base of candle.

7. Burn candle down just enough to place a tea light candle in top for burning.

White Rose Taper

Photo on page 72.

Things Needed
- Acrylic paint: as desired
- Paintbrush: round, small
- Taper candle

Instructions
1. Using acrylic paint, paint small roses in a random pattern on candle. Roses are made by applying a small dot of paint and then adding comma strokes of paint around the dot. Small leaves are then painted.

2. Begin painting roses at the bottom and work up to the top. Prop candle up to dry.

Glitter Taper

Photo on page 72.

Things Needed
- Glitter: fine
- Glue: craft
- Taper candle

Instructions
1. Using a glue bottle with a pointed tip, create a squiggle pattern beginning at bottom of candle.

2. Every 4-5" inches, stop and pour glitter over wet glue. Shake off excess glitter. Prop candle up to dry.

Papered Taper

Photo on page 72.

Things Needed
- Craft knife
- Glue: découpage
- Japanese paper
- Paintbrush: flat
- Taper candle

Instructions
1. Using flat paintbrush, spread découpage glue on candle. Lay paper down on flat surface. Wrap candle in paper.

2. Using craft knife, trim excess paper carefully at top and bottom.

Monogram Candle
Things Needed
- Acrylic paint: dk. blue
- Charm: metal, 2" oval with center opening
- Copper or aluminum sheeting: 3" square
- Glue: industrial-strength
- Masking tape
- Paintbrush: flat; old
- Paper towels
- Pencil
- Pillar candle
- Rubber bands
- Silver leafing
- Silver leafing adhesive
- Stylus
- Tin snips
- Transfer paper

Instructions

1. Place two strips of masking tape 2" apart in a spiral up candle. Using an old paintbrush, paint a thin layer of silver leafing adhesive in 2" areas between tape strips. Allow to dry for at least 30 minutes. Apply silver leafing over adhesive. Remove tape.

2. To make monogram charm, use a stylus to trace around outside of metal charm onto metal sheeting. Using tin snips, cut out metal ⅛" inside traced line.

3. Using transfer paper and pencil, transfer desired monogram letter onto center of metal.

4. Place cut metal on a flat surface and press monogram design into metal using stylus. Trace over letter with stylus using firm pressure.

5. Using industrial-strength glue, attach monogrammed metal to charm piece. Allow to dry. Bend monogram charm slightly to fit surface of candle. Apply diluted dk. blue acrylic paint over charm. Wipe off immediately with a paper towel, leaving some paint in indentations for an antiqued look.

6. Glue monogram to side of candle with industrial-strength glue. Rubber bands may be used to hold charm in place until glue has dried.

Sealing Wax Candle

Photo on page 73.

Things Needed
- Charms: silver filigree (4)
- Glue: industrial-strength
- Matches
- Paintbrush: old
- Pillar candle
- Ribbon: ⅞"-wide, sheer with metallic details (1 yd.)
- Sealing wax stamp
- Sealing wax stick
- Silver leafing
- Silver leafing adhesive
- Stapler and staples

Instructions

1. Using an old paintbrush, paint a thin layer of silver leaf adhesive over front sides of charm. Allow to dry for at least 30 minutes. Apply silver leafing over adhesive.

2. Place center of ribbon at back of candle about 1" from candle top. Make tuck in ribbon to allow sides to angle down. Open stapler and staple ribbon in place on back of candle. Bring ribbon ends around to front of candle. Cross ends and staple in place.

3. Using industrial-strength glue, attach charms in a diamond shape to candle center over top of ribbon. Staples bent in "U" shapes may also be pressed into candle to further secure charms. Allow glue to dry 24 hours.

4. Lay candle down with charms at top. Light sealing wax stick with a match and drip at center of charms until wax pools to the size of a quarter. Press immediately with sealing wax stamp.

"Candle Lite"

Photo on page 73.

Things Needed
- Bead: silver seed
- Needlenose pliers
- Staples
- Wire: 26 gauge, silver (6')

Instructions

1. Using pliers to crimp and form letters, bend wire into desired words.

2. To attach wire words to candle, straighten several staples and then form them into a "U" shape. Push staples into candle over top of wire shapes. To dot the letter "i", thread a silver seed bead onto a staple "U" and press in place.

Seashell Candle

Things Needed
- Dried flowers: as desired
- Glue: craft
- Glue gun and glue sticks: low temperature
- Pillar candle
- Seashells: as desired
- Spanish moss

Instructions

1. Using finger tips, evenly spread craft glue around bottom two-thirds of candle. Press Spanish moss onto glued area. Allow to dry for a few minutes.

2. Beginning with the largest flat seashells and using glue gun, apply glue to inside shell edges and attach to moss covered area. Add remaining shells filling in space as desired.

3. Using glue gun, attach small pieces of dried flowers between shells.

Chapter Seven:
Decorating Candle Containers

Golden Fishbowl

Things Needed
- Candle: as desired
- Fishbowl: glass
- Glue: découpage
- Newspaper
- Masking tape
- Paintbrush: flat
- Paper towels
- Spray paint: metallic gold
- Tissue paper

Instructions
1. Wrap paper towels around outside of fishbowl covering completely. Secure in place with masking tape. Place fishbowl on newspaper. Spray inside top of fishbowl lightly with metallic gold spray paint. Paint should be darker at edge and fade slightly into bowl.

2. Tear tissue paper into 1½" pieces. Remove tape and paper towels from fishbowl.

3. Using flat paintbrush, spread a thin layer of découpage glue in about a 3-4" area inside fishbowl. With right sides toward glue, apply tissue paper pieces overlapping as necessary to cover inside of fishbowl completely. Press pieces down with paintbrush to release air bubbles. Allow to dry.

4. Paint another coat of découpage glue over the top of tissue paper to seal.

5. Place candle in fishbowl.

Leaf Candle Holder

Photo on page 78.

Things Needed
- Acrylic paints: beige; dk. brown; deep brown-red; lt. tan
- Candle holders (2)
- Crackle medium
- Dried leaves: as desired
- Glue: craft; découpage
- Gold and copper leafing
- Gold leaf adhesive
- Paintbrushes: 1" flat; round, small
- Paper towels
- Rubbing alcohol
- Spray sealer: satin
- Taper candles (2)

Instructions
1. Using rubbing alcohol and paper towels, clean surface of candle holders completely.

2. Using flat paintbrush, spread a thin coat of découpage glue onto candle holders. Allow to dry.

3. Paint one candle holder using beige paint and one using dk. brown paint.

4. Using flat paintbrush, apply craft glue to backs of leaves and adhere them to candle holders. Make certain there are no bubbles or loose edges. Do not apply crackle medium to surface of leaves. Once

glue has dried, cover candle holders with crackle medium following manufacturer's instructions. Allow crackle medium to dry.

5. Reversing colors, paint beige paint over dk. brown candle holder and dk. brown over beige candle holder. As paint dries, cracks will appear.

6. Using small round paintbrush, apply random areas of gold leaf adhesive to both candle holders. Allow adhesive to dry for at least 30 minutes. When adhesive has dried, apply small bits of gold and copper leafing over areas of adhesive following manufacturer's instructions.

7. Using flat paintbrush, lightly dry brush rims of candle holders with deep brown-red paint. Rub some of paint off with a paper towel to soften look.

8. Dilute one drop of lt. tan paint with 1 tablespoon water. Lightly dab mixture over light areas, painting, and crackle. Wipe paint off immediately with paper towel.

9. Spray candle holders with three light coats of satin spray sealer.

10. Place taper candles in candle holders.

77

Leaf Drip Plates

Things Needed
- Acrylic paints: as desired
- Glue: craft
- Paintbrushes: flat; sponge
- Paper sack: brown
- Scissors: craft
- Silk leaves: as desired
- Votive candles

Instructions
1. Using craft scissors, cut paper sack into pieces slightly larger than size of silk leaves. Using slightly diluted glue and flat paintbrush, layer and adhere 4-5 pieces of cut brown paper.

2. Apply full strength craft glue to back of one leaf and attach it to layered brown paper. Cut paper around leaf outline. Glue a matching leaf to the back of paper. When matching leaves cannot be found, back of paper may be sponge painted with acrylic paint to match front of leaf.

3. While leaf is still pliable, form into desired shape.

4. Using flat paintbrush, paint edges of leaves. Add color to centers if desired.

5. Place votive candles on leaves.

Butterfly Hurricane

Things Needed
- Candle holder for pillar candle: glass
- Dish soap
- Etching cream: glass
- Etching stencils: glass, butterfly
- Glue gun and glue sticks
- Hurricane shade: glass, 12"
- Masking tape
- Pillar candle
- Scissors: craft
- Silk flowers and greenery: as desired
- Wire edge ribbon: 1½"-wide (3 yds.)

- Wire cutters
- Wreath frame: wire, 12" dia.

Instructions

1. Clean all glass pieces with dish soap and water. Dry all glass pieces.

2. Following manufacturer's instructions, apply glass etching stencils to outside of hurricane shade. Tape off edges of stencils using masking tape.

3. Apply thick layer of etching cream to each stencil, working quickly. Etching cream should not remain on shade for longer than one minute.

4. Rinse cream off shade under running water. When all cream is washed off, remove stencils and tape. Dry shade.

5. Wrap ribbon around wire wreath frame, tacking starting end in place with glue gun. Overlap ribbon slightly and continue wrapping until frame is covered. Secure ribbon end with glue. Using craft scissors, trim excess ribbon if necessary.

6. Using wire cutters, clip stems from silk flowers and pull leaves from stems. Discard stems. Arrange flowers and leaves around ribbon-covered frame. Glue in place as desired.

7. Place wreath over a pillar candle on an inverted candle holder. Place hurricane over candle.

Victorian Hurricane
Photo on page 81.
Things Needed
- Candle holder: glass, 6"
- Cardboard: 2" x 4"
- Dish soap
- Hurricane shade: glass, 12"
- Glass paint: frost

- Glue gun and glue sticks
- Lace: 2½"-wide (⅜ yd.)
- Masking tape
- Paintbrush: liner, old
- Pillar candle
- Plate: glass, 8"
- Scissors: fabric; craft
- Silk leaves: small
- Silk roses: small
- Wire cutters
- Wire-edge ribbon: 1½"-wide (½ yd.)

Instructions
1. Clean all glass pieces with dish soap and water. Dry all glass pieces.

2. Place lace inside top of hurricane, trim with fabric scissors if necessary to make ends meet. Tape lace in several places to secure.

3. On outside of hurricane, paint with an old liner brush and frost glass paint using lace inside as a pattern. When design is completed, remove lace and tape from inside hurricane.

4. Place hurricane on plate. Cut piece of cardboard for floral base to fit the curve of the hurricane and plate.

5. Using glue gun, adhere one end of ribbon to cardboard. Wrap ribbon around cardboard, covering completely. Secure end in place with glue. Glue same

lace used for hurricane design around edge of ribbon covered cardboard base. Gather lace slightly while gluing. Using wire cutters, cut silk roses and leaves from stems. Glue on silk roses and leaves as desired.

6. Turn glass plate face down on a flat surface. Place candle in candle holder and candle holder in center of plate. Place hurricane shade over plate. Glue floral arrangement to back of plate

Frosted Hurricane
Photo on page 81.
Things Needed
- Dish soap
- Glass spray: frosted
- Hurricane base: glass
- Hurricane shade: glass, 12"
- Pillar candle

Instructions
1. Clean all glass pieces with dish soap and water. Dry all glass pieces.

2. Following manufacturer's instructions, spray inside of hurricane and hurricane base with frosted glass spray. Do not touch inside of hurricane or frosted spray will become smudged.

3. Place pillar candle on base. Place hurricane shade over candle.

Gauze Shade

Photo on page 83.

Things Needed
- Candle stand
- Copper wire: 18 gauge (1⅜ yds.)
- Gauze: 16" x 6½", white
- Glue: fabric
- Metal rings: 2"; 5"
- Needles: hand-sewing
- Spray paint: bronze
- Tea bags
- Thread: coordinating
- Votive or tea light candle

Instructions
1. Using craft scissors, cut 16" x 6½" piece of gauze. Tea dye gauze and tightly twist it, leaving gauze twisted until dry.

2. Cut four 8" lengths of thin copper wire. Wrap each wire around small metal ring 7-8 times, leaving a 5" length extending. Wrap tip of each extended end once around 5" metal ring. Space wires evenly to create a shade form.

3. Using bronze spray paint, paint candle stand and metal shade form.

4. Hand-stitch short ends of gauze together with a ¼" seam. Fold one long edge of gauze under ¼". Wrap folded end around 2" metal ring at top of metal shade form and hand-stitch in place with a running stitch. Gather stitches to make fabric fit ring.

5. Roll unfinished bottom end of gauze up slightly, securing it in place with fabric glue applied with fingers. Glued hem should be uneven.

6. Place votive candle or tea light candle in candle stand.

Ruffled Ribbon Shade

Photo on page 83.

Things Needed
- Candle stand with glass shade
- Glue gun and glue sticks
- Ribbons: 1⅜"-wide, wire-edge, sheer (4 yds.)
- Scissors: fabric
- Votive or tea light candle

Instructions
1. Remove glass shade from candle stand.

2. Fold sheer wire-edge ribbon under horizontally ¼". Glue to secure to top of glass shade. Wrap ribbon around shade overlapping rows. Continue until entire glass shade is covered.

3. Using fabric scissors, trim off excess ribbon. Glue ribbon end to inside bottom edge of glass shade.

4. Place shade on stand over votive or tea light candle.

Ribbon & Braid Shade

Photo on page 83.

Things Needed
- Things Needed for Ruffled Ribbon Shade
- Braiding: ½"-wide (1 yd.)
- Fringe: ½"-wide (½ yd.)

Instructions
1. Remove glass shade from candle stand.

2. Using fabric scissors, cut sheer ribbon into pieces to fit vertically from top to bottom of glass candle shade. Glue and wrap ribbon ends to shade, overlapping ribbon. Glue fringe around bottom of shade. Glue two layers of braiding to top of shade and one layer of braiding over fringe around bottom.

3. Place shade on stand over votive or tea light candle.

Découpage Shade

Photo on page 85.

Things Needed
- Candle stand with glass shade
- Craft knife
- Glue: découpage
- Paintbrush: flat
- Paper: handmade
- Votive or tea light candle

Instructions
1. Remove glass shade from candle stand.

2. Tear handmade paper into small pieces and adhere to glass candle shade with découpage glue in a collage style. If the paper is different on front and back, alternate pieces of paper by gluing some face down and others face up.

3. When entire outside of shade is completely covered, trim edges of paper shade with craft knife.

4. Using flat paintbrush, spread découpage glue on entire outside surface of shade. Allow to dry completely.

5. Place shade on stand over votive or tea light candle.

Writing Shade
Photo on page 85.
Things Needed
• Candle stand with glass shade
• Craft knife
• Glue: découpage
• Paintbrush: flat
• Paper: parchment, tan
• Scissors: craft
• Votive or tea light candle

Instructions
1. Remove glass shade from candle stand.

2. Enlarge Pattern A at copy center. Place pattern on tan parchment paper. Using craft scissors, cut pattern out.

3. Working quickly using flat paintbrush, spread découpage glue on back of parchment pattern. Smooth pattern down around shade overlapping slightly in back. Use fingers to smooth out wrinkles or bubbles.

Pattern A   Enlarge 190 %

4. Using craft knife, trim edges of paper shade.

5. Spread découpage glue on entire outside surface of shade. Allow to dry completely.

6. Place shade on stand over votive or tea light candle.

Stamped Shade

Photo on page 85.

Things Needed
- Candle stand with glass shade
- Craft knife
- Embossing powder: clear
- Glue: découpage
- Heat gun
- Paintbrush: flat
- Paper sack: 15" x 6", brown
- Pigment stamping inks: as desired
- Rubber stamps: petroglyph
- Votive or tea light candle

Instructions

1. Remove glass shade from candle stand.

2. Soak brown paper sack with water. Squeeze excess water from paper and wad paper up into a ball, wrinkling as much as possible. Set paper aside for a few minutes.

3. Spread paper out to dry, but do not smooth out wrinkles. When paper is dry, stamp it as desired using petroglyph stamps, pigment inks, and clear embossing powder. Set embossing powder with heat gun.

4. Do not allow découpage glue to get on stamped surface of paper. Using flat paintbrush, spread découpage glue to underside of paper and adhere it to the glass shade. Use fingers to smooth out wrinkles or bubbles.

5. Using craft knife, trim edges of paper shade.

6. Place shade on stand over votive or tea light candle.

Tin Punch Shade

Photo on page 89.

Things Needed
- Candle stand with glass shade
- Fabric paint: gold
- Glue: industrial-strength
- Hammer
- Masking tape
- Metal sheeting: 38 gauge, gold finish
- Nails or awl
- Newspapers or magazines
- Pencil
- Sandpaper
- Scissors: scallop-edge
- Votive or tea light candle
- Wire: decorating, gold

Instructions

1. Remove glass shade from candle stand.

2. Enlarge Pattern A and Pattern B on page 88 at copy center. Place Pattern A on wrong side of metal sheeting. Tape in place. Place metal sheeting and embossing pattern on top of a stack of newspapers or magazines to protect work area. Trace over pattern with pencil using strong pressure. This will transfer pattern into metal.

When embossing is complete, remove pattern and tape.

3. Turn metal right side up and tape Pattern B onto right side of metal. Press with pencil into punch marks to transfer pattern. Remove pattern and punch holes in metal according to pattern using a nail or awl and a hammer. Make certain this is done on a stack of newspapers or magazines.

4. Using sandpaper, distress metal slightly causing some of the metal to come off. Using scallop-edge scissors, cut out shade pattern on metal.

5. Wrap metal around glass shade and secure in place with industrial-strength glue.

6. Wrap gold decorating wire in a criss-cross pattern around the stem of the candle stand. Secure wire in place by twisting until wire tightens.

7. Using fabric paint, decorate candle base with swirls and polka-dots. Allow fabric paint to dry thoroughly before handling.

8. Place shade on stand over votive or tea light candle.

Pattern A   Enlarge 220 %

Pattern B   Enlarge 220 %

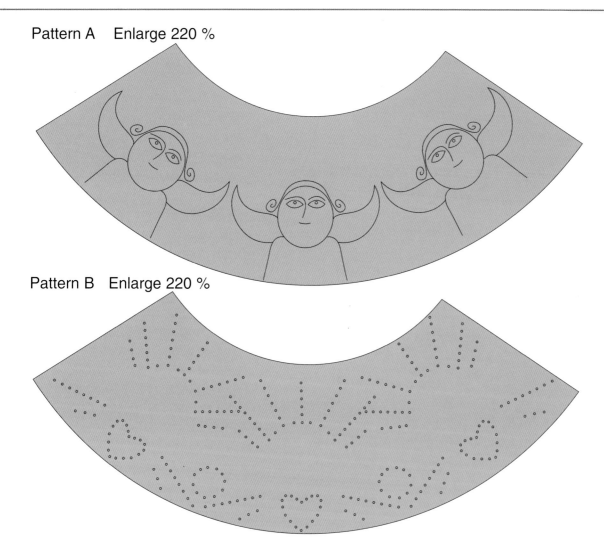

Pansy Shade
Things Needed
• Candle stand
• Copper mesh material: 5½"-wide (½ yd.)
• Metal ring: 5"
• Needles: darning
• Scissors: craft
• Velvet flowers and leaves
• Votive or tea light candle

Instructions
1. Using craft scissors, cut copper mesh material to measure 16" in length.

2. Pull a long piece of copper wire from extra mesh. Tread darning needle with the wire. Sew a running stitch along one long edge of mesh and gather to fit small circle at top of candle stand. Sew gathered side to small circle, wrapping gathered edge of mesh over while sewing in place.

3. Place velvet flowers in between layers of mesh arranging as desired. Overlap raw ends of mesh and sew together.

4. Gather and sew bottom end of mesh 5" metal ring, wrapping mesh around ring while stitching.

5. Place votive or tea light candle in candle stand.

Beaded Shade

Photo on page 89.

Things Needed

• Beads: ³⁄₁₆", gold (50); ³⁄₁₆", blue (80); ⅛", red (190)
• Candle stand
• Metal rings: 1¾"; 5"
• Needlenose pliers
• Newspapers
• Spray paint: gray hammered metal
• Votive or tea light candle
• Wire: 14 gauge (12'); 18 gauge (12')
• Wire cutters

Instructions

1. Using wire cutters, cut 14 gauge wire into four 24" lengths and four 10½" lengths. Find centers of 24" lengths and make a slight bend. This point will be the top center point of each loop shape. Using pliers when needed, bend each side down from center point to form a 2"-long 1"-wide loop. Grasp both wires at the bottom of loop with pliers and twist together three times. Bend ends out at bottoms and form into scroll shape. See Diagram A. Repeat with each 24" length.

Diagram A

2. Bend each 10½" length of wire into an "S" shape about 3" long. The top scroll should be smaller than the bottom. See Diagram B.

Diagram B

3. Cut twenty-four 3" lengths of 18 gauge wire to use as connections for wire shapes. To make connections, loop wire tightly around four times and then twist together on the inside of shape to secure. Trim ends and crimp with pliers.

4. Using connecting wires, connect tops of each looped wire section evenly around 1¾" metal ring. Connect each scroll end on looped wire to 5" metal ring. See Diagram C.

Diagram C

Adjust bend of scrolls if necessary to fit around ring. Wire "S" sections between loop sections.

5. Protect working surface with newspapers. Using gray hammered metal spray paint, paint wired shade.

6. Cut four 12" lengths of wire to attach gold beads. Wrap around and twist one end of one wire to top of looped section. Thread a bead onto the other end of wire and slide up to fit snugly against inside looped section. Wrap wire around loop, and thread another bead onto wire. Position second bead about ¼" from first bead, then wrap wire around loop again. Repeat until row of gold beads is completed inside loop. Wrap and twist wire to secure end. Trim if necessary. Repeat for remaining loops.

7. Cut four 15" lengths of 18 gauge wire. Attach one end of one wire to upper peak of triangle shape at bottom of shade between scroll shapes on looped sections.

8. Thread blue bead onto wire and slide it into place at top of triangle. Wrap wire around and thread another bead on; wrap again. Continue to complete one row inside triangle. Fill in triangle shape with beads by weaving beads and wire around and through the first row of beads and wire.

Continue until shape is filled. See Diagram D. Repeat for remaining triangle shapes.

Diagram D

9. Cut one 7½" and one 18" piece of 18 gauge wire. Crimp wires ½"in from ends and thread each wire with red beads.

10. Wrap 7½" beaded wire around top of shade and 18" beaded wire around bottom of shade. Adjust each to fit and twist ends of wires in place to secure. Use several lengths of 18 gauge wire to wire beaded wires in place along top and bottom of shade. Trim ends.

Finished Section

11. Place shade on stand over votive or tea light candle.

See title page for close-up and other colorful cylinder patterns.

Colorful Cylinders
Things Needed
- Enamel paints: as desired
- Masking tape
- Paintbrushes: flat; round; liner
- Paper towels
- Pillar candles
- Scissors: craft
- Vases: glass, cylinder, 10½" x 3½" (4)

Instructions
1. Enlarge Patterns A-D on pages 92-93 at a copy center.

2. Trim copies as needed.

Place copies inside vases and tape to temporarily secure.

3. Using paintbrushes and enamel paints, paint sections of cylinders, applying lines, flowers, vines, leaves, and dots as indicated by patterns. Darker and lighter shades of paint can be applied to give leaves and flowers dimension. Shapes may be outlined with brown or black paint. Thin squiggles of paint may be applied with a liner brush to connect floral designs in a lattice pattern.

4. Remove any mistakes with a damp paper towel while paint is still wet.

5. To cure paint on cylinders, follow paint manufacturer's instructions for curing glass.

6. Place pillar candles in cylinders.

Paint patterns with colors to match any decor.

Apply tole painting patterns in holiday motifs to cylinders.

Pattern A   Enlarge 135%

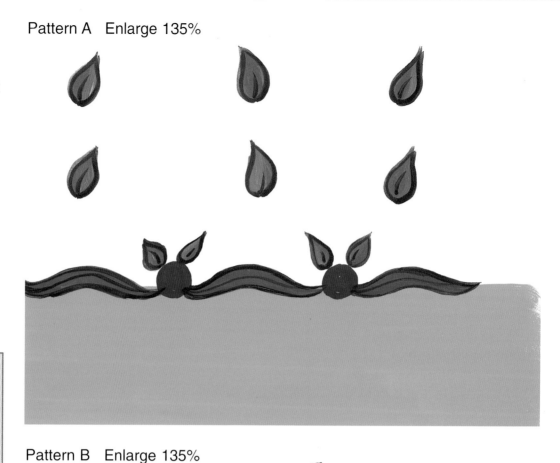

Pattern B   Enlarge 135%

Pattern C   Enlarge 175%

Pattern D   Enlarge 175%

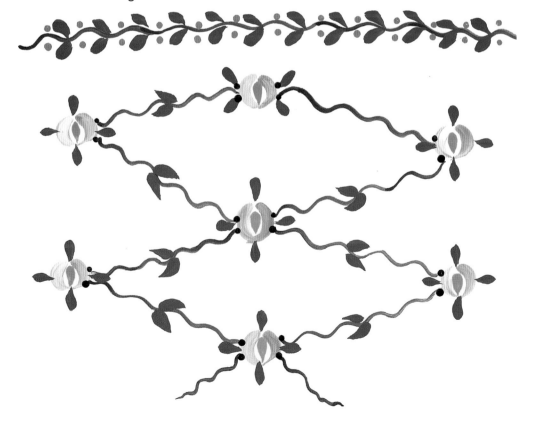

Victorian Globes

Things Needed (for one globe)

- Buckram: 2" square
- Candle globe
- Cotton balls
- Fabric: organza, 15" square
- Fabric paint: metallic
- Glue: craft
- Needles: hand-sewing
- Newspapers
- Pinking sheers
- Ribbons: ¾"-wide (1 yd.); 1½"-wide (½ yd.); 1½"-wide (3½" scrap); 1"-wide (¾ yd.); 1½"-wide (⅜ yd.)
- Rubber bands
- Scissors: fabric
- Stamens: double-ended
- Thread: coordinating
- Votive candle
- Wire: 24 gauge

Instructions

1. Using pinking sheers, trim edges of organza fabric square. Working over newspapers, apply metallic fabric paint to edges of organza. Allow to dry.

2. Place candle globe in center of organza square. Draw corners up to top of globe and slip rubber band around lip of globe to hold fabric in place. Pull gathers evenly around globe. Tie 1 yd. length of ribbon into a bow around globe, covering rubber band.

3. Cut 16" length from ½ yd. length of ribbon. Mark and stitch as shown in Diagram A.

Diagram A

4. Use gathering stitch with a stitch length of ¼". Pull stitching tight, knot, and trim thread. Apply a small amount of craft glue to flower "tails", pinch them together, and turn to back of three petal flower as shown in Diagram B. Glue flower to globe over ribbon bow.

Diagram B

5. Gather stamens and wrap with wire to secure. Glue to globe just under three petal flower.

6. Fold and glue 3½" ribbon scrap as shown in Diagram C. Use glue to secure base of leaf and glue to globe.

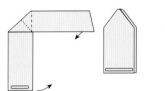

Diagram C

7. Cut five 3½" lengths and one 6" length from ¾ yd. length of ribbon. Fold and glue 3½" lengths into petals as shown in Diagram D.

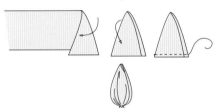

Diagram D

8. Draw ¾" circle on buckram and glue flower petals at even intervals around circle. To make flower center, glue the ends of remaining 6" ribbon together with right sides of ribbon facing. Run ribbon right side out. Using a gathering stitch, stitch around one long edge of ribbon. Pull stitching tight, knot, and trim thread. Stuff ribbon with a cotton ball and gather-stitch other long side of ribbon as shown in Diagram E.

Diagram E

9. Glue flower center to center of petals on buckram. Carefully cut out buckram circle, without cutting petals. Glue flower to globe.

10. Cut three 3½" lengths from ⅜ yd. length of ribbon. Fold and glue into three gathered rosebuds as shown in Diagram F. Glue gathered rosebuds to globe.

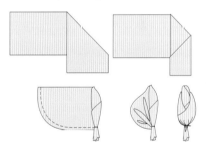

Diagram F

11. Place votive candle in globe.

Note: A variety of globes can be constructed using varied colors and textures of ribbons and organza.

Floss Wrapped Vases

Photo on pages 96-97.

Things Needed
- Beads: as desired
- Charms: as desired
- Double-sided tape
- Glue: craft
- Lace: flat
- Overdyed floss or cording
- Pillar candles
- Ribbons: as desired
- Scissors: fabric
- Vases: glass, cylinder

Instructions
1. Using fabric scissors, cut ribbons and lace to fit around vases. Using double-sided tape, attach ribbon and lace to vases as desired. Use craft glue to attach ribbon and lace overlaps.

2. Glue floss end to top of ribbon on overlap. Wrap floss around vases in a variety of ways to create designs as desired. Additional strips of ribbon or lace can be applied on top of floss.

3. Using craft glue, add beads and charms to corded areas as desired.

4. Place pillar candles in vases.

Bronze Vase

Photo on page 99.

Things Needed
- Acrylic decorating paste
- Acrylic paints: flesh tone; bronze
- Antiquing gel: brown
- Decorating bag with #16, #5 decorating tips
- Masking tape
- Paintbrush: flat
- Pickling gel
- Pillar candle
- Sponge
- Spray paint: white
- Spray sealer
- Tracing paper
- Toothbrush: old
- Vase: glass, cylinder

Instructions
1. Photocopy Pattern A at copy center or trace it onto tracing paper. Using masking tape, tape pattern inside vase.

2. Fill decorating bag fitted with decorating tip #16 with acrylic decorating paste. Following pattern taped inside vase, apply decorating paste to vase beginning in center of design at #1. Switch to decorating tip #5 to make the long "S" shaped scroll on outline at #6.

3. Reposition pattern and repeat three more times for a total of four patterns on vase. Direction of pattern can be

Pattern A Actual size

alternated to create one set of scrolls pointing up and one set pointing down.

4. Using #5 decorating tip, freehand small dots and swirls on bottom of vase as desired. Allow vase to dry undisturbed for several hours. For best results, allow to dry overnight.

5. Using white spray paint, spray entire outside of vase.

6. Using sponge, apply flesh tone paint to outside of vase, completely covering all designs. While the paint is still wet, lightly sponge on bronze paint.

7. Dilute pickling gel slightly. Using flat paintbrush, paint it onto raised design areas.

8. Using an old toothbrush, splatter paint the vase with brown antiquing gel.

9. Spray vase with sealer.

10. Place pillar candle in vase.

Flowers & Lace Vase

Photo on page 99.

Things Needed

- Acrylic decorating paste
- Acrylic paints: cream; lt. gray; lt. moss green
- Aluminum foil
- Antiquing gel: brown
- Cloth: clean, dry
- Decorating bag with #102, #65 decorating tips
- Glue: découpage
- Lace: 2"-wide with square panels
- Paintbrushes: flat; round
- Pillar candle
- Scissors: fabric
- Spray paint: white
- Spray sealer
- Vase: glass, cylinder

Instructions

1. Using fabric scissors, cut lace into ten 2" squares.

2. Using flat paintbrush, spread découpage glue on back of lace squares and adhere them to vase as shown in photograph on page 99.

3. Fill decorating bag fitted with decorating tip #102 with acrylic decorating paste. Using decorating bag, make five petal flowers on vase between lace squares.

4. To make petals, hold the wide end of decorating tip away and apply paste in a quarter circle motion.

5. Switch to decorating tip #65 to make two small leaves for each flower. Allow flowers and leaves to dry undisturbed for several hours. For best results, allow to dry overnight.

6. Using white spray paint, paint outside of vase.

7. Place equal amounts of cream, lt. gray, and lt. moss green paints onto a piece of aluminum foil. Dip a round paintbrush into each of the colors and then dab it onto vase. Continue until entire surface of vase is covered.

8. Working in one small area at a time, apply slightly diluted antiquing gel to vase. Rub off excess with a clean dry cloth.

9. Spray vase with sealer.

10. Place pillar candle in vase.

Wallpaper Vase

Things Needed

- Acrylic decorating paste
- Acrylic paint: as desired
- Decorating bag with #13 decorating tip
- Dish soap
- Glitter: as desired
- Glue: découpage, reverse
- Paintbrush: flat
- Pillar candle
- Scissors: craft
- Vase: glass, cylinder
- Wallpaper scrap

Instructions

1. Clean vase with dish soap and water. Dry vase.

2. Using craft scissors, cut wallpaper to fit inside of vase.

3. Using flat paintbrush, spread a thin coat of reverse découpage glue to front of wallpaper piece. Adhere wallpaper to inside of vase.

4. Tint half a jar of decorating paste with acrylic paint to match wallpaper.

5. Using decorating bag fitted with a #13 decorating tip, fill one-third of the way with tinted decorating paste. Write name or phrase on vase and make a border as shown in the photograph on page 101.

6. Immediately sprinkle glitter over decorating paste. Allow paste to dry for several hours. For best results, allow to dry overnight.

7. Place pillar candle in vase.

Overdyed Floss Pot

Things Needed
- Glass rocks: unpolished
- Glue: craft
- Masking tape
- Overdyed floss: 4-5 skeins
- Ribbon scraps: as desired
- Scissors: fabric
- Terra-cotta flowerpot
- Votive candle

Instructions

1. Using fabric scissors, cut skeins of floss in half at one end and separate skeins into groups of 3-4 strands of floss. Lay each strand section out flat. There should be 8-9 sections in all.

2. Cut assorted lengths of various ribbons and loop them randomly around sections of floss. Secure ribbon loops in place with craft glue. Leave one section of floss plain, without ribbon wrapping.

3. Use fingertips to spread craft glue over bottom fourth of pot. Wrap one ribbon wrapped section of floss around glued section of pot, tucking in floss ends. Continue applying glue and applying sections of floss until pot is covered in floss and ribbons up to beginning of rim. Spread glue on pot rim and adhere a piece of ribbon around it. Apply more glue to center of ribbon wrapped rim and then wrap section of plain floss around rim.

4. Cover hole in bottom of pot with masking tape. Fill with glass rocks.

5. Place votive candle in center of pot.

Woven Ribbon Pot

Things Needed
- Acrylic paint: as desired
- Buttons: old
- Glue gun and glue sticks
- Masking tape
- Paintbrush: flat
- Scissors: fabric
- Terra-cotta flowerpot
- Votive candle
- Wire-edge ribbons: ½"-wide, 2 colors (2½ yds. each)

Instructions

1. Using fabric scissors, cut one color of ribbon to fit around pot sides. Cut 36" length of the same color ribbon to make bow. Cut remaining second color of ribbon to weave between horizontal ribbon strips.

2. Using flat paintbrush, paint top band of pot with acrylic paint.

3. Wrap horizontal strips of ribbon around pot securing in place at ends with glue gun. Weave vertical strips of ribbon through horizontal strips. Wrap bottom ends of vertical ribbons around edge of pot and secure to pot bottom with glue. Tie 36" length of ribbon around top of pot in a bow.

4. Cover hole in bottom of pot with masking tape. Fill pot with buttons.

5. Place votive candle in center of pot.

Crackle Pot

Things Needed
- Acrylic paints: 2 colors as desired
- Crackle medium
- Glue: industrial-strength
- Masking tape
- Metal jewelry leaf
- Paintbrush: flat
- Spray sealer
- Terra-cotta flowerpots (2)
- Votive candle

Instructions

1. Slightly bend metal leaf to fit side of pot. Using industrial-strength glue, attach leaf to side of pot.

2. Using flat paintbrush, paint pot and leaf with one color of acrylic paint. Allow to dry, then apply crackle medium. Paint second color of acrylic paint over crackle medium. Spray pot with sealer.

3. Break second pot into small pieces.

4. Cover hole in bottom of pot with masking tape. Fill pot with broken pot pieces.

5. Place votive candle in center of pot.

Jewelry Pot

Photo on page 102.

Things Needed
- Acrylic paint: as desired
- Buttons, charms, beads, jewels: as desired
- Glue: craft
- Masking tape
- Papiér-mâché: instant
- Terra-cotta flowerpot
- Votive candle
- Waxed paper
- Wire cutters

Instructions

1. Using wire cutters, clip backs off assorted buttons.

2. Following manufacturer's instructions, mix papiér-mâché. Add enough acrylic paint to papiér-mâché mix to achieve desired color.

3. Spread papiér-mâché over outside of pot ½" thick. Set pot down on waxed paper and spread a coat of papiér-mâché inside of pot.

4. Before papiér-mâché has set up completely, dip backs of assorted buttons, charms, beads, and jewels into craft glue and press into papiér-mâché. Start with larger objects, then fill in space with smaller objects.

5. Allow project to dry for 2-3 days.

6. Cover hole in bottom of pot with masking tape. Fill pot with buttons, charms, beads, and jewels.

7. Place votive candle in center of pot.

Curly Candle Hanger

Things Needed
- Beads: tubular, 1" (2); faceted, 2⅜" (5)
- Needlenose pliers
- Votive candle
- Votive candle holder
- Wire: 14 gauge (4½ yds.); 18 gauge (⅜ yd.)
- Wire cutters

Instructions

1. Using wire cutters, cut 2 pieces of 14 gauge wire 25" long. Leaving 6½" of wire extending, form one piece of wire into a 2½"-diameter circle. Start at bottom of votive holder. Place wire circle around votive holder. Where wire meets, grasp with pliers and twist together, forming two twists. Bend 6½" end down and into a scroll shape. Bend longer end up, curve slightly out, and bend into a scroll shape. Repeat technique with second wire. Place wire circles together with twists and scrolls at opposite sides. Fasten together in 3-4 places with small loops of 18 gauge wire. See Diagram A.

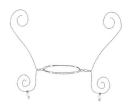

Diagram A

2. Cut two 2" pieces of 14 gauge wire and slide a 1" tubular glass bead onto each wire. Using pliers, bend each wire into a loop at each end of beads. These will be used as connectors.

3. Cut 27" length of 14 gauge wire. Mark center of wire with a small crimp. Bend each end into a scroll shape. With crimp mark at center top, bend center of wire into a heart shape. At lower point of heart, grasp both wires and twist together, forming two twists. Bend scrolled ends out to same width as scrolls on candle holder. Connect two scrolled sections with beaded wire connectors made in step 2. See Diagram B.

Diagram B

4. Cut two 12" lengths of 14 gauge wire. Bend one wire into an "S" shape with scrolls at each end. Repeat for other wire, making shape identical on each. See Diagram C.

Diagram C

5. Cut two 1" pieces of 14 gauge wire. Connect top of heart to each scroll shape forming 1" wires into loops for connectors. See Diagram D.

Diagram D

6. Cut 18" length of 14 gauge wire. Mark center of wire and bend both ends down to form 1½"-long top loop. Using needlenose

pliers grasp wires at bottom of loop and twist together to form two twists. Bend ends out, down, and into scroll shapes. See Diagram E.

Diagram E

7. Cut five 1" lengths of 18 gauge wire and thread 2⅝" bead onto each. Bend one end of wire around lower curve of top section forming a loop. Bend other end of beaded wire around top bend of "S" scroll shape. Repeat with other wire, making shape identical on each side.

8. Bend one end of each remaining beaded wire into a loop. Attach one to bottom of each scroll shape near candle and one to center of heart.

9. Place votive candle in holder.

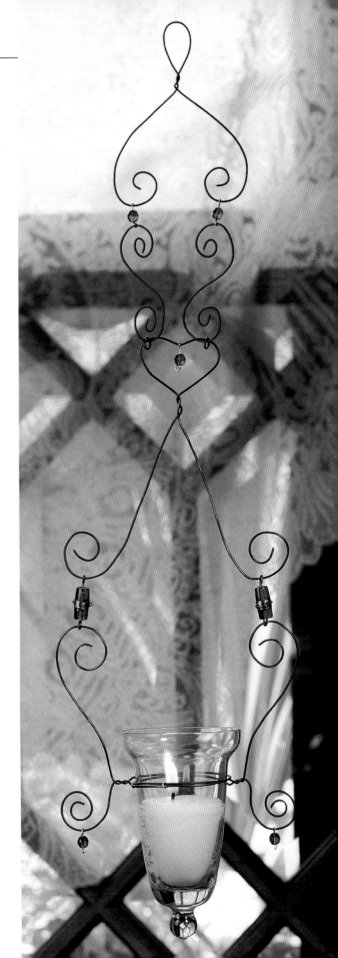

Baluster Candlesticks

Things Needed
- Balusters: old (3)
- Candle cups (3)
- Drill and drill bit: size of candle cups
- Scroll saw
- Taper candles (3)

Instructions

1. Using scroll saw, cut balusters to desired heights. Vary heights for visual impact. Cut a small amount from bottoms of balusters to level them so balusters can stand.

2. Find center top of each baluster. Using drill, drill a hole there to fit the diameter of the candle cup.

3. Place candle cups into drilled holes.

4. Place taper candles in candle cups.

Hope & Happiness Egg

Photo on page 107.

Things Needed
- Things Needed for Melting Wax on pages 19-21
- Egg: two-part, unglazed porcelain
- Glue gun and glue sticks
- Pencil
- Permanent calligraphy pen: metallic gold
- Permanent marker: metallic gold
- Ribbons: 3⅛"-wide, gold metallic élan (7"); ⅞"-wide, sheer metallic stripe (7")
- Ribbon rose: metallic gold
- Scissors: fabric
- Wick: square, primed
- Wick tab

Instructions
1. Separate egg halves. Stretch élan over top half of egg. Turn under edge of rim, and cut away excess using fabric scissors. Using glue gun, spread glue in a thin layer to secure élan in place.

2. Glue one end of sheer ribbon to underside of egg rim at center back. Pull ribbon over top of egg and glue in place on opposite side.

3. Glue rose in place on center top of egg.

4. On egg bottom, pencil in words such as Joy, Hope, Love, Happiness, and Dreams. Go back over penciled letters with a gold calligraphy pen. Keep the pen flat during lettering. Allow lettering to dry between words to reduce chance of smears.

5. Use a metallic gold marker to draw a gold line around upper and lower edges of bottom half of egg.

6. See Wick Tabs on page 13. Place wick and wick tab into bottom center of egg half. See Melting Wax on pages 19-21. Melt wax. Pour melted wax into egg bottom.

Ribbon Flower Egg

Photo on page 107.

Things Needed
- Things Needed for Melting Wax on pages 19-21
- Charms: angel wings (2)
- Glue gun and glue sticks
- Gold braid (⅝ yd.)
- Ribbon flowers: gold
- Scissors: fabric
- Wick: square, primed
- Wick tab

Instructions
1. Using glue gun, attach ribbon flowers to egg as desired. See photo on page 107. Glue angel wing charms together like butterfly wings.

2. Wrap gold braid around wings to hide glue. Glue wings to top of egg.

3. Cut gold braid into two 11" lengths. Glue one around edge of top egg and one around edge of bottom egg.

4. See Wick Tabs on page 13. Place wick and wick tab into bottom center of egg half. See Melting Wax on pages 19-21. Melt wax. Pour melted wax into egg bottom.

Canisters with Jewels

Things Needed
- Bead wax
- Canister jars: glass (3)
- Fabric paints: as desired
- Glue: découpage
- Paintbrush: flat
- Rhinestones: as desired
- Scissors: craft
- Sparkle glaze
- Spoon
- Wick: wire core, primed
- Wrapping paper

Instructions
1. Using craft scissors, cut wrapping paper designs or panels to fit sides and tops of glass jars.

2. Using flat paintbrush, spread découpage glue onto canister. Use fingers to smooth out wrinkles or bubbles.

3. Embellish jars as desired using fabric paints and sparkle glaze. While fabric paint is still wet, press rhinestones into paint as desired. The paint will act as a glue, holding the rhinestones in place.

4. Using spoon, insert bead wax in canisters.

Gold Charm Votive
Things Needed
- Beads: glass, as desired
- Charms: copper leaf
- Pliers
- Votive candle
- Votive candle cup
- Wire: 28 gauge, gold
- Wire cutters

Instructions
1. Using wire cutters, cut three 16" lengths of wire. Twist all three wires together at one end. Randomly add a few beads to wires. Measure 1½" and twist wires together again. Add more beads, measure 1½" and twist wire again. Continue two or more times until twisted wires are long enough to fit around votive candle cup. Twist wire ends together to secure wires in a beaded ring.

2. Spread wires apart between twists. Add additional curls and twists in separated wires.

3. Cut five 2½" lengths of wire. Thread beads and leaf charms onto each length of wire. Wrap wires around twisted sections of beaded ring. Twist ends of wires to secure to ring.

4. Set beaded wire ring over top of votive candle cup. Bend top wires over top of votive candle cup to hold beaded ring in place.

5. Place votive candle in cup.

Blue Beaded Votive
Things Needed
- Beads: glass, square (30); as desired (30)
- Charms: as desired
- Glue: industrial-strength
- Needles: beading
- Thread: clear
- Votive candle
- Votive candle cup
- Wire: 28 gauge, gold
- Wire cutters

Instructions
1. Using wire cutters, cut 15" length of wire. String enough square glass beads onto wire to fit around top of votive candle cup. Twist wire ends together to secure in a ring. Trim excess wire if necessary.

2. Using beading needle, string assorted beads and charms onto clear thread and tie randomly to wire between square glass beads. Using

industrial-strength glue, glue ring of square glass beads to top of votive candle cup.

3. Place votive candle in cup.

Photograph Votive
Things Needed
- Copper foil tape: silver backed
- Glass pieces: ⅞" x ⅝" (8)
- Glue: industrial-strength
- Patina: copper
- Paintbrush: old
- Photos: ⅞" x ⅝" (4)
- Scissors: craft
- Soldering flux
- Soldering iron and solder
- Soldering wire: rosin core
- Votive candle
- Wire: 26 gauge, gold
- Wire cutters

Instructions
1. Place one photo between two glass pieces. Apply copper foil tape around edges of glass pieces. Make certain tape extends slightly onto faces of both glass pieces.

2. Using an old paintbrush, apply a small amount of soldering flux onto the foil tape. If too much flux is applied, it may seep between glass layers.

3. Hold heated solder iron in one hand and solder wire in other. Working as carefully and quickly as possible, apply hot solder to copper foil tape.

Beads or pools of solder may form, giving the project a rustic look. If that look is undesirable, beads or pools of solder may be heated and carefully removed.

4. Using wire cutters, cut one yard of rosin core soldering wire. Bend wire in half and twist halves together. Twist enough wire to fit around the top of the votive candle cup with ½" overlap. Twist ends of wire together to secure, creating a ring.

5. Cut four random lengths from 26 gauge wire and fold them over rosin core ring spacing evenly. Twist wires to secure. Using industrial-strength glue, glue rosin core ring to top of votive candle cup. Allow to dry upside down.

6. Using soldering iron, attach each glass covered photo to ends of 26 gauge wires with a bead of solder.

7. Paint over wire, rosin, and soldered areas with copper patina.

8. Place votive candle in cup.

Red Charm Votive

Photo on page 111.

Things Needed
• Acrylic paint: gold metallic
• Charms: heart (4)
• Glue: industrial-strength
• Paintbrush: old
• Soldering wire: rosin core
• Thread: clear
• Votive candle
• Votive candle cup
• Wire: 26 gauge, gold
• Wire cutters

Instructions

1. Using wire cutters, cut one yard of rosin core. Bend wire in half and twist halves together. Twist enough wire to fit around top of the votive cup with ½" overlap. Twist ends of wire together to secure, creating a ring.

2. Cut four random lengths from 26 gauge wire and fold them over rosin core ring spacing evenly. Attach one charm to each wire. Twist wires to secure. Using industrial-strength glue, glue ring to top of votive candle cup. Allow to dry upside down.

3. Using an old paintbrush, paint over wire, rosin, and charms with copper patina.

4. Place votive candle in cup.

Green Charm Votive

Photo on page 111.

Things Needed
• Charms: bells (5)
• Jump rings (5)
• Patina: copper
• Paintbrush: old
• Votive candle
• Votive candle cup
• Wire: 28 gauge, gold
• Wire cutters

Instructions

1. Using wire cutters, cut 15" length of wire. Randomly twist wire in all directions until it fits snug around votive candle cup. Secure wire by knotting.

2. Using an old paintbrush, paint over charms with patina.

3. Attach one charm to each jump ring. Attach one jump ring with charm over knotted wire. Randomly attach other four jump rings with charms onto twisted wire. Secure jump rings by squeezing them shut.

4. Place votive candle in cup.

Chapter Eight:
Decorating with Candles

Tips for Displaying and Storing Candles

▪ Place candles where they are the focal point of the room and where the most can be made from the light they offer.

▪ Display candles out of drafts. Drafts will cause candles to burn unevenly and to drip when being burned.

▪ Always consider safety when displaying and using candles.

▪ Display candles in a way that also stores them. See photo on left.

▪ Store candles flat in a cool, dark place to prevent warping and fading.

Appropriate Candle for Time and Place

Candles do not need to be reserved for special occasions. Their beauty can be enjoyed daily. The following pages are filled with ideas on decorating with candles.

113

Traditional candle holders are only one way to display candles. Common household objects can be used to create an endless variety of unexpected candle holders. This antique lamp base makes a surprisingly fun candle holder. The candle is simply inserted into the light socket. The amount of illumination provided by this candle is doubled by displaying it in front of this rustic mirror.

A plant stand makes a charming candle holder, perfect for outdoor entertaining. These floral candles can be purchased or made using home grown flowers and greenery. To create these candles, see Double Mold Candles on page 44. Candles lit on a still night can bring fragrance and mystery to a garden party.

Candles can be used to create any mood imaginable. Candles can be lavish and formal or rustic and whimsical. These plump pear candles add a touch of country charm to their surroundings. Displayed on top of flowerpots in a nostalgic flower crate, this tempting fruit looks sweet enough to eat.

Fire and ice make a striking combination. This simple candle becomes dazzling when surrounded in ice and brightly colored flowers. To create this unique center piece, place a candle into milk or juice carton. The carton should be taller than the candle. It should also be a snug fit around the sides. Place fresh flowers around the candle and then carefully pour water into the container. Stop pouring water when it comes within 2" from the top of the candle. Place carton in the freezer overnight.

To display the candle, dip container in warm water, remove from water, and then carefully peel the carton away. Place ice candle on a plate, to catch the water as the ice melts. The plate can also be embellished with fresh flowers for an added touch.

Candles are enchanting wherever they are placed. The possibilities for potential candle holders are limitless. Consider using a candle to lend a dreamy feel to a simple fishbowl. This tall, slim pillar candle is pleasing to the eye and safe for the fish. Make certain to use a dripless candle to keep wax from falling into the water.

Floating candles can add radiance and romance to any background. When displaying floating candles, do not waste the space beneath. Fresh or silk flowers, marbles, glass shards, or even glass trinkets can be placed in the water below the candle for a unique presentation. One of these glass cylinders contains a full-bloomed begonia and the other a glass frog. Use a memento or keepsake to design a one-of-a-kind display.

Candles and candleholders can be purchased or painted in colors to match any home decor. These candles were sprayed with gold spray paint and paired with gold leafed candle holders to match the gold accents in the table. A length of gold cord was then wrapped and tied around the vase turned candle holder to complete this bold look.

No matter what the color scheme or theme, there is a candle to match. These natural candles add a feeling of freshness to this country china cupboard. A candle with a corresponding color and feel is often just the attention to detail a room needs.

Any occasion becomes more festive when candles are used. Add fun to a rootbeer float party with cupcake-topped glasses. A variety of cheerful candles makes these simple cupcakes extraordinary.

Miniature novelty candles or candleholders can brighten any birthday. Candles can be purchased to fit a party theme, or to reflect the personality of the guest of honor. After the singing, wishing, and blowing are done, candles can be kept as mementos of the occasion.

Candle light by moonlight can create a sense of romance and mystery. This simple outdoor candle features a sphere constructed with chicken wire. This creative candle cover creates fascinating shadows that add interest with minimal effort.

Decorating a twilight gathering with lawn torches is a simple way to disperse light. This ornate floral torch is surprisingly easy to construct using inexpensive materials. To make the torch, secure an old cardboard thread cone to the end of a wooden dowel. Wrap the cone and a small section of dowel with floral tape. Then, use a glue gun to attach artificial magnolia petals to the top of the cone. A colorful braid or rope can also be added to embellish the dowel. A votive candle inserted into a candle cup is placed at the top of the torch. Magnolia petals do not stand up well when exposed to the elements, so the torch should be stored inside when not in use.

Metric Equivalency Chart

mm-millimetres cm-centimetres
inches to millimetres and centimetres

inches	mm	cm	inches	cm	inches	cm
⅛	3	0.3	9	22.9	30	76.2
¼	6	0.6	10	25.4	31	78.7
½	13	1.3	12	30.5	33	83.8
⅝	16	1.6	13	33.0	34	86.4
¾	19	1.9	14	35.6	35	88.9
⅞	22	2.2	15	38.1	36	91.4
1	25	2.5	16	40.6	37	94.0
1¼	32	3.2	17	43.2	38	96.5
1½	38	3.8	18	45.7	39	99.1
1¾	44	4.4	19	48.3	40	101.6
2	51	5.1	20	50.8	41	104.1
2½	64	6.4	21	53.3	42	106.7
3	76	7.6	22	55.9	43	109.2
3½	89	8.9	23	58.4	44	111.8
4	102	10.2	24	61.0	45	114.3
4½	114	11.4	25	63.5	46	116.8
5	127	12.7	26	66.0	47	119.4
6	152	15.2	27	68.6	48	121.9
7	178	17.8	28	71.1	49	124.5
8	203	20.3	29	73.7	50	127.0

yards to metres

yards	metres	yards	metres	yards	metres	yards	metres	yards	metres
⅛	0.11	2⅛	1.94	4⅛	3.77	6⅛	5.60	8⅛	7.43
¼	0.23	2¼	2.06	4¼	3.89	6¼	5.72	8¼	7.54
⅜	0.34	2⅜	2.17	4⅜	4.00	6⅜	5.83	8⅜	7.66
½	0.46	2½	2.29	4½	4.11	6½	5.94	8½	7.77
⅝	0.57	2⅝	2.40	4⅝	4.23	6⅝	6.06	8⅝	7.89
¾	0.69	2¾	2.51	4¾	4.34	6¾	6.17	8¾	8.00
⅞	0.80	2⅞	2.63	4⅞	4.46	6⅞	6.29	8⅞	8.12
1	0.91	3	2.74	5	4.57	7	6.40	9	8.23
1⅛	1.03	3⅛	2.86	5⅛	4.69	7⅛	6.52	9⅛	8.34
1¼	1.14	3¼	2.97	5¼	4.80	7¼	6.63	9¼	8.46
1⅜	1.26	3⅜	3.09	5⅜	4.91	7⅜	6.74	9⅜	8.57
1½	1.37	3½	3.20	5½	5.03	7½	6.86	9½	8.69
1⅝	1.49	3⅝	3.31	5⅝	5.14	7⅝	6.97	9⅝	8.80
1¾	1.60	3¾	3.43	5¾	5.26	7¾	7.09	9¾	8.92
1⅞	1.71	3⅞	3.54	5⅞	5.37	7⅞	7.20	9⅞	9.03
2	1.83	4	3.66	6	5.49	8	7.32	10	9.14

Index